Economic Thought
Volume 3, Issue 2, 2014

Table of Contents

In line with the objectives of the World Economics Association, this journal seeks to support and advance interdisciplinary research that investigates the potential links between economics and other disciplines as well as contributions that challenge the divide between normative and positive approaches. Contributions from outside the mainstream debates in the history and philosophy of economics are also encouraged. In particular, the journal seeks to promote research that draws on a broad range of cultural and intellectual traditions.

Economic Thought accepts article submissions from scholars working in: the history of economic thought; economic history; methodology of economics; and philosophy of economics - with an emphasis on original and path-breaking research.

Website http://et.worldeconomicsassociation.org
Contact eteditor@worldeconomicsassociation.org

Managing editor
Kyla Rushman

Co-editors
Sheila Dow, UK, University of Stirling, and Canada, University of Victoria
John King, Australia, La Trobe University and Federation University Australia
John Latsis, UK, University of Reading
Alejandro Nadal, Mexico, El Colegio de Mexico
Annalisa Rosselli, Italy, University of Rome Tor Vergata

Editorial board
Richard Arena, France, University of Nice-Sophia Antipolis
Robert U. Ayres, France, INSEAD
Daniel W. Bromley, USA, University of Wisconsin at Madison
Bruce Caldwell, USA, Duke University
Victoria Chick, UK, University of London
David C. Colander, USA, Middlebury College
John B. Davis, Netherlands, Universiteit van Amsterdam
Jean-Pierre Dupuy, France, École Polytechnique and Stanford University
Donald Gillies, UK, University of London
Tony Lawson, UK, University of Cambridge
Maria Cristina Marcuzzo, Italy, La Sapienza, Università di Roma
Stephen Marglin, USA, Harvard University
Manfred Max-Neef, Chile, Universidad Austral de Chile
Deirdre McCloskey, USA, University of Illinois at Chicago
Erik S Reinert, Norway, The Other Canon
Alessandro Roncaglia, Italy, La Sapienza, Università di Roma
Irene van Staveren, Netherlands, Erasmus University

ISSN 2055-6314 (print)
ISSN 2049-3509 (online)
ISBN 978-1-84890-170-4

Published by College Publications on behalf of the World Economics Association
Sister WEA open-access journals: *World Economic Review* and *Real-World Economics Review*

College Publications
Scientific Director: Dov Gabbay
Managing Director: Jane Spurr

http://www.collegepublications.co.uk

Original cover design WEA.
Printed by Lightning Source, Milton Keynes, UK

-

J.M. Keynes, F.A. Hayek and the Common Reader

Constantinos Repapis, Institute of Management Studies, Goldsmiths, University of London, UK
c.repapis@gold.ac.uk

Abstract

This paper gives an account of the debate between F.A. Hayek and J.M. Keynes in the 1930s written for the general public. The purpose of this is twofold. First, to provide the general reader with a narrative of what happened, and pointers to further reading which are accessible to the non-specialist. Second, to discuss how academics can fruitfully bridge the gap between their specialist work and the public without reducing complex themes into one-dimensional narratives. I use the Keynes vs. Hayek debate as a case study on how this may be achieved.

Keywords: J.M. Keynes, F.A. Hayek, Keynesianism, neo-Austrian theory, common reader

1. Introduction

> 'A study of the history of opinion is a necessary preliminary to the emancipation of the mind. I do not know which makes a man more conservative – to know nothing but the present, or nothing but the past' (Keynes, 1926).

As I quote these lines a Youtube video titled '"Fear the Boom and Bust" a Hayek vs. Keynes Rap Anthem' uploaded on January 23, 2010 has more than 4,700,000 views, and has spawned another two videos, one titled 'Fight of the century, Keynes vs. Hayek round two' with 2,700,000 views and 'Hayek's Gift' with 190,000 views.[1] This is not the usual material that goes viral on Youtube. But, somehow bizarrely, it is not that surprising. Both Hayek and Keynes have been so much in the public debate from the start of the current economic crisis that their views, theories and lives have become subjects of popular interest. In this spirit the BBC has recently completed a three-part series titled *Masters of Money*, where Stephanie Flanders looked at the life, work and influence of Keynes, Hayek and Marx.

---

[1] I want to thank Jonathan Haas for first bringing this video to my attention, and the many students who have asked to discuss it ever since.

It is not only visual media that has picked up this trend. Journalist Nicholas Wapshott wrote *Keynes Hayek, the clash that defined Modern Economics* (2011). The book has been read widely and has been reviewed both in the public (Clarke, 4 February 2012; Congdon, 29 February 2012; Koehn, 23 October 2011) and academic press (Cochran, 2011; Cornish, 2013; Davidson, 2012; Patrick, 2012; Skidelsky, 2013; Steele, 2012; Tankersley, 2012). Furthermore, other writers have worked on similar topics (Hoover, 2003; White, 2012; Yergin and Stanislaw, 2002). Also, a number of new monographs have investigated related themes, for example, the rise of neoliberalism until the financial crisis (Jones, 2012) or the fortunes of free market ideology after the Great Depression (Burgin, 2012). These books, some academic studies and others more journalistic in character, are written in a variety of styles, and by authors with diverse backgrounds. Nevertheless, they are all written at least partly for the general public, and not only for the specialist.

There are a number of interesting questions that this literary and other media activity brings to the fore. One is a question of the usefulness of any such exercise beyond entertainment. A usual charge is that historical parallels between the current crisis and the great depression are based on facile generalisations. I do not agree with this view, but, more importantly, I do not find it relevant to what these and other similar texts that are available to the general public actually do. These texts focus on key episodes that bind personal histories with broader socio-economic conditions.[2] It is no surprise that they are popular. By their ability to move from the specific to the general they give meaning to a period of history that the general reader finds interesting in its own right, and useful in understanding the ideas that shape modern political discussion.

Such an activity is deeply democratic and goes against the compartmentalisation and cloistering of knowledge that increasingly defines academic study in the humanities and social sciences. Informing the public about these central intellectual figures, their work, and how their work was shaped by their beliefs and personal histories is a way to add to the public dialogue. In essence this argument is not new. The common reader tradition in English literature has analysed how the creation of a mass reading public from the 19th century onwards shapes and is shaped by what is written. Altick writes 'the history of the mass reading public is, in fact, the history of English democracy seen from another angle' (Altick, [1957] 1998, 3). Furthermore, celebrated literary figures from Dr

---

[2] Lawrence White explains how such stories employ a non-linear historical narrative approach with flashbacks and other digressions that brakes up tight chronological sequencing. At the same time these digressions should not scramble events in such a way that the narrative the author is trying to create confuses the reader. White, in what is, I think, the best description of how this approach works, calls it '*Tarantinoesque* – only with more polite language and slightly less bloodshed' (White, 2012, p. 3). This insight opens up an interesting and related discussion: How do we construct effective narratives? Are there techniques which are acceptable and others which are not? I will not attempt to deal with this set of questions in this paper, taking as a given the existence of a narrative, and building on that. But questions on how to build storylines and how the storyline affects the scheme proposed in this paper are important and merit further investigation.

Johnson to Virginia Woolf have seen the common reader with a sympathetic eye, accepting that he has a say in the final distribution of 'poetical honours' (Johnson, 1866, p. 614). Equally, the general public today expects that economic theory and theorists will advance arguments and advise both the public and governments on policy issues implying that this is, to some degree, the reason for research. And while a full-scale investigation of the habits, interests and motivations for this 'common reader of economics' remains a desideratum in academic study,[3] it can be argued that these popularisations perform a useful function in a democratic society.[4]

There is, however, a danger. That danger is a descent into over-simplification and caricature. Instead of making the public debate richer and deeper, these stories can simply infuse it with drama and historical colour. Is there a way to avoid this? And how can we do it without reducing what we have to say to an academic argument detached from the public debate, or worse, to a scholastic exercise that excites only our professional peers?

I have no fully formed answer to this question, and I suspect there isn't a general answer that could cover the wide array of topics that connects historians of economic thought with the reading public. Instead, in this paper, I explore a specific approach in the context of the Hayek vs. Keynes intellectual duel that is already in the public spotlight. My approach is based on the conviction that no single text can do justice to such a rich theme, with its complicated technical analysis and ideologically charged episodes. Instead, I utilise the following device. In the next section I build a simple and brief narrative that captures what I consider to be the main aspects of this debate, so that the reader can get a general idea of the intellectual battle. Then in section three I build a commentary on the narrative that guides the reader through a list of readings that he can go and explore if he wishes, so that he can gain a more substantial understanding of these issues. At another level, this commentary effectively works against the simple story

---

[3] A first study on this elusive 'economics common reader' can be found in Lamm (1993). Related work has been carried out by methodologists and historians of economic thought on popularisations of contemporary economics. The development of a literature called 'Economics for Fun' has been the subject of a number of recent studies (see e.g. Aydinonat, 2012; Backhouse, 2012; Fleury, 2012; Maki, 2012; Vromen, 2009). This literature focuses on popularisations of mainstream economics and the various methodological and other questions that arise from this activity. In Repapis (2013) I discuss the importance of writing for the common reader for heterodox economics as seen through the work of G.C. Harcourt. But at this juncture it is important to draw the distinction between what the popularised texts say, and what is understood, perceived, or seen as the message by their intended audience. Jonathan Rose in his preface of *The Intellectual Life of the British Working Classes* (2010) notes that academic readers analyse texts or popular culture by reacting to these texts as if they are the intended audience – which they are not. This is why there is a need to gather evidence, not only on what people read, but how they read it, why they do so and what do they take from this reading, if we are to get a deeper understanding of the 'common reader of economics'.

[4] An older literature following Webb (1955) focuses on issues of increasing literacy in the early 19th century and the efforts of the upper middle class to introduce 'proper' political economy to the working classes. This brings to the fore issues of ideology and class frictions that are central to any discussion on why, how and for whom economic ideas get popularised. Therefore, the relation between economic theory, popularisations, social stratification and democratic debate is not a simple one, and needs to be further analysed.

constructed, and it allows different readers to interact in their own way with the narrative of the previous section. Some satisfied with the simple précis may leave it at that. Others may wish to explore specific aspects of the debate that they found interesting. Others still, may use the commentary to detach themselves from the certainty a simple narrative gives, and realise, to some extent, the complexity of the theme and natural limits of the narrative provided.

Even if we agree with all of this, we can argue that this device holds nothing new. Books, both academic and more journalistic in character, have bibliographies and footnotes, some of them quite voluminous. Isn't that effectively the same thing? I do not think so. The problem is the following: if the book is written in such a way as to give substantial referencing and commentary in the text with long footnotes problematising every generalisation the author is making, it will lose its appeal *vis-à-vis* the common reader. If the supporting structure is too lean, then it cannot take the reader very far. In all cases the text frames the literature review in a way that I find too limiting, as it can only deal with points directly raised by the main narrative itself. Freeing the texts from this symbiotic existence allows more freedom for the writer who may try, at times, to add more and more detail to a heaving storyline, and the reader from the unpleasantness of skipping or skim reading parts of the text as his patience runs out. The most important reason, however, is that it re-establishes a balance between the author, the reader, and other writers that is democratic and aims to inform rather than merely argue.[5]

How successful this approach is in solving the problems previously outlined in establishing a link that is deep and thought-provoking between the writer and the general public is something that will be further discussed in the conclusion of this paper. But, before that, we visit the Hayek vs. Keynes debate one more time.

2. Keynes vs. Hayek: A (Very) Brief Overview of the Debate

In this brief overview I do not intend to flesh out in detail the theories of both economists. Instead, in the interests of brevity, I will focus on Hayek's theory of money and the trade cycle, and bring in Keynes as the other side of the argument, the contrasting view. I concentrate on Hayek because Keynes's theoretical output is in some sense more varied. First, because he formulated more than one theoretical scheme in the 1930s, and

---

[5] It should be mentioned that a couple of books that aim to inform the public have a section on further reading with a brief commentary, as for example we find in Skidelsky (2010). My suggestions in this paper are in line with this practice. In fact, they provide arguments why such sections are necessary, why they should be longer, and give more information about reading sources and how they connect to what the writer argued in his narrative, instead of being akin to brief lists of books and articles. Therefore, this is a plea to authors to use this further reading section in a more imaginative fashion, even if this leads them to question the narratives constructed in their main text, and reveal to the reader inevitable incongruences.

second, because Keynes's theoretical output has had a broader and more complex interpretative tradition in macroeconomics than Hayek's.

To set the stage, it is worth remembering that the 1920s had been seen by contemporary politicians and economists as a period of relative prosperity. Professor Lionel Robbins writes in his book *The Great Depression* published in 1934 '[the 1920s was] a period, indeed, which ... can be seen to have been one of the biggest booms in economic history. Trade revived, incomes rose. Production went ahead by leaps and bounds. International investment was resumed on a scale surpassing even pre-war dimensions. The stock exchanges of the more prosperous centres displayed such strength that speculation for a rise seemed a more certain path to a secure income than all the devices of ancient prudence' (Robbins, 1934, p. 7). This was not to last for long. The period from 1929 to 1933 upset the confidence that economists and politicians had had in the free market for most of the latter part of the 20th century. As early as 1934, Robbins proclaimed: 'there have been many depressions in modern economic history, but it is safe to say that there has never been anything to compare with this. 1929 to 1933 are the years of the Great Depression' (Robbins, 1934, p. 11). Economists found themselves in a crisis they did not anticipate, but almost immediately recognised it as a singular event in modern economic history.

How did the economic profession respond to these unprecedented events? Keynes through a series of popular articles, pamphlets, and his book *A Treatise on Money*, published in 1930, was trying to provide a new theoretical base that would be in line with these events. He was still groping with the ideas that would bear fruit in 1936 and would be elucidated in one of the most important economic books of the century, *The General Theory of Employment, Interest and Money*. Equally, the London School of Economics (LSE) was in turmoil.

In the early 1930s the LSE had no economist of equal stature and authority to Keynes. Professor Robbins decided to bring from Austria a theorist who could add to the school's research profile, putting it on par with Cambridge. This was none other than Friedrich von Hayek. On January 1931 Hayek would give four lectures on the Austrian theory of the trade cycle that would be the opening shots in the upcoming battle between these two theorists. Later that year these lectures would be published in book form with the title *Prices and Production*. Arguably, this became the most celebrated book by Hayek in the 1930s.

Prices and Production develops a theory that attempts to explain a typical trade cycle in such a way that it reconciles the Austrian theory of value with the macroeconomic phenomena of the 1930s. This means that Hayek tried to build on existing economic theory, and especially on the analytical foundations of the Austrian school of economics, in order to show that this theoretical framework can be extended to explain extreme events like the Great Depression.

A simple view of how a typical trade cycle works can be seen in figure 1. The diagrams in figure 1 depict two distinct scenarios. In both cases we start from an equilibrium position which has interest rate (r), and a volume of loanable funds (A). At point (a), the amount of saving people are willing to supply at this interest rate equals firms' demand for funds for investment projects. On the left diagram we have an autonomous increase in saving, where people decide to voluntarily save more of their income. On the right we have an increase in the supply of money in the economy, where the central bank, or the commercial banks, decide to increase credit to the producers/ entrepreneurs, while none of the underlying real factors of the economy have changed. This means that people have not decided to save more than before. Instead this gap between what people intend to save and the volume of investment is filled by the credit expansion.

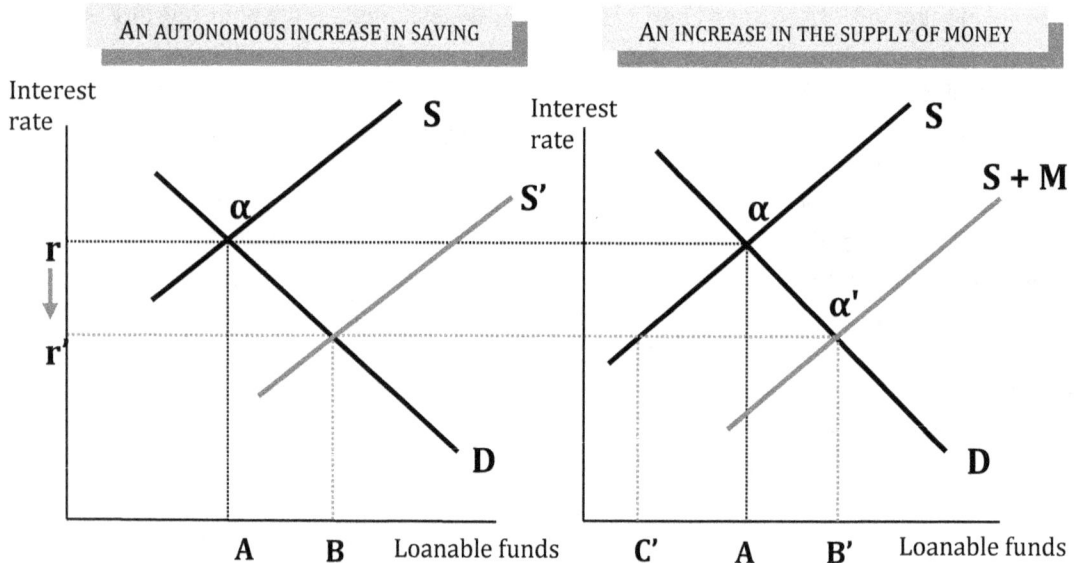

AN AUTONOMOUS INCREASE IN SAVING   AN INCREASE IN THE SUPPLY OF MONEY

Figure 1.

Source: Garrison, R. (1996) The Austrian Theory: A Summary, in *The Austrian Theory of the Trade Cycle* edited by M. Ebeling, Alabama: L.V. Mises Institute, p. 113

We first consider what happens when there is an autonomous increase in saving by the population. It is important to note that in Hayek's view of the world savings are always funnelled to increased opportunities for investment. Therefore, when people decide to save a greater part of their income, it necessarily follows that we have a shift of the supply curve. This is because we have a change in the amount people intend to save for every level of the interest rate. Given the decreasing profitability of investment plans; so that at lower interest rates more plans can yield profit; the demand for loans is a negative function of the interest rate. The new intersection of the curves shows that the outcome of this autonomous increase is to permanently lower the interest rate and permanently increase the volume of investment plans materialising. Thus, through thrift, the future abounds with goods. Today's increase in saving leads to a more prosperous future, as lower interest rates allow producers to reorganise production in such a way that it will yield more consumption goods in the future. This new production process is more 'sophisticated' or to put it in standard terminology more 'roundabout'. It was lower interest rates that made setting up this new process economically viable, and made economic growth possible.

Next, we consider what happens in the second case, when the shift in the supply schedule is not the outcome of thriftiness, but of increased credit supplied by the commercial banks or by the central bank. Hayek noted that when commercial banks, in their pursuit for profit in an uncertain environment, or the central bank in its wish to reap political gains, abuse their role as intermediaries between the public that saves and the entrepreneurs that invest this saving, what follows is a trade cycle.

Therefore, when the central bank increases the supply of credit in the economy, the new short period equilibrium position is at B'. But this is not a stable equilibrium. Soon enough, as prices start to rise, and some of the investment plans are in arrears, banks start to realise that they do not have the stream of savings to finance this increased activity in the investment sector. In fact, the credit expansion that depressed the interest rate also decreased the wish of the individuals to save. Therefore, we are still on the old supply schedule and, at the new interest rate (r'), individuals would wish to reduce the amount they save to point C'.

As the economy adjusts to these new conditions it becomes increasingly apparent that the level of saving that individuals wish to hold captured by (C') does not correspond to the level of investment in this economy, captured by (B'). Overnight the interest rate rises as the banks try to safeguard their reserves from depletion. At the same time banks start to cut lending. The crisis stage of the trade cycle is imminent. The 'irrational exuberance' that created the boom, sowed the seeds for the crisis, and nothing that the government can do can alter the course of events now. During the crisis stage of the cycle, and as the economy reorganises itself, we observe the common phenomena of increased unemployment, decreased production, and wage deflation. The reason why we have both unemployment and unused capital is because there is a misalignment between what the market wants in consumer and producer goods, and what its existing capital structure can deliver. Thus, according to Hayek, physical capital may appear underutilised, but the reason for this phenomenon is that its economic use has decreased, as it was built to deliver a specific array of goods. What it can produce is no longer in demand, hence its economic value has diminished, and workers remain unemployed as the old production processes shut down and the new ones are yet to be fully functional.

If the government, through the central bank, responds by continuing to keep an artificially low interest rate so as to avert the crisis, it is only buying time. The government cannot avoid the crisis forever because then the value of paper money would be reduced to zero. Therefore, the longer the crisis is averted, the bigger the economic *mal*coordination created by government intervention, and the more violent the crisis stage of the cycle, when eventually reached. For Hayek, the government displays wisdom when it lets the market operate unhindered and opportunism when it interferes.

Hayek in his analysis of the trade cycle as sketched in *Prices and Production* had started from a position of long period equilibrium. In that book he tried to outline a theory that would encompass both the period of prosperity and that of depression. Keynes's approach and reaction to the crisis was radically different. Keynes viewed the crisis stage of the cycle not as a necessary correction for the irresponsibility and malcoordination of the boom, but as a crisis of confidence that tipped the delicate balance of a market economy. For stability to be re-established it is necessary for the government to intervene. Keynes wrote in December 1933, in an open letter to President Roosevelt, 'I lay overwhelming emphasis on the increase of national purchasing power resulting from governmental expenditure which is financed by loans and is not merely a transfer through taxation, from existing incomes; nothing else counts in comparison with this' (Keynes, [1982] 2012, p. 293).

To understand how this position is rooted in theory we need to look ahead at the arguments that were to develop in the *General Theory*. There, the neo-classical causal relationship which underlines Hayek's theory breaks down. The analysis does not start from the independent saving decisions of individuals, and then, from these actions/decisions all other variables are determined. Instead, we start from the money rate on interest, which is determined in the financial market, and given the prospective yield of capital at any point in time, we have a volume of investment. This, through the multiplier process, determines income and the level of saving in the economy. Therefore, causality is reversed! Investment determines income and income determines the level of saving in the economy, and not *vice versa*. This is because when people earn more, they are able to consume and save more. Keynes was afraid of the vicious cycle in which reduced income leads to unemployment, unemployment causes lower consumption, and reduced consumption further decreases income. He writes in the *General Theory*, 'the traditional analysis has been aware that saving depends on income but it has overlooked the fact that income depends on investment, in such a fashion that, when investment changes, income must necessarily change in just that degree which is necessary to make the change in saving equal to the change in investment' (Keynes, [1936] 1973, p. 184).

Hayek's world was still one in which saving dictated the interest rate, and the level of investment, given the profitability of investment plans. For Hayek, what was observed during the crisis was the abandonment of investment plans because people wanted to consume more, and it was more often than not, the central bank with its opportunistic behaviour of making money cheap that caused the crisis. From this he deduced, not only that the government had no good role to play in this affair, but also, that the crisis is important in order to bring those who thought that opportunism could triumph over prudence, back in line.

Therefore, Hayek and Keynes took very different paths in their efforts to combine neoclassical economic theory with the events of the Great Depression. Hayek's theory focused on the cyclical nature of prosperity and depression, making him pessimistic about ascribing to the government any corrective role. Keynes perceived the crisis as an inherent flaw of the capitalist system. In the *General Theory,* the government was seen as a stabilising force in an inherently unstable world. For Keynes the mechanisms of the classical system operated when it was business as usual but failed to apply in periods of economic turmoil.

Their differences did not end there. Hayek saw another disturbing prospect in ascribing to the government an ever-increasing economic role. Could it be that the emerging intellectual consensus in the 1930s and 1940s of the need for more government intervention and more central planning as the only therapy to the inherent flaws of capitalism was putting society on a path towards socialism?

This prospect motivated Hayek in writing *The Road to Serfdom*, arguably his most widely read book. With its publication in 1944 we have a first idea of the grander conflict that was to develop after the war between these two broad views of social organisation and the limits of market activity outside the Soviet Bloc.

Hayek, in all his writings from the 1920s until the end of his life, displayed a strong dislike for anything that could restrict the freedom of action of the individual. He believed that individuals are absolutely sovereign. He could not morally accept any kind of social organisation where man is not permitted to pursue his own ends unhindered. In *The Road to Serfdom* he wrote 'economic life is the administration of the means for all our different ends. Whoever takes charge of these means must determine which ends shall be served, which values are to be rated higher and which lower, in short what men should believe and strive for' (Hayek, 1944, p. 121). This is why he feared the growing power of the state.

Keynes agreed in principle with Hayek. He wrote to Hayek when he read his book: 'morally and philosophically I find myself in agreement with virtually the whole of it; and not only in agreement, but in deeply moved agreement' (Keynes, [1977] 2012, p. 385). By 1940 Hayek appeared equally convinced that the differences between Keynes and himself were not a full-blown dispute on the form of economic organisation that societies should strive for. Keynes was not a socialist, and shared with Hayek a deep commitment to the liberal capitalist tradition of the West. This became evident in the correspondence following the publication of *How to Pay for The War* in February 1940. Hayek, in a letter to Keynes on the 3th of March 1940, wrote 'It is reassuring to know, that we agree so completely on the economics of scarcity, even if we differ on when it applies' (published in Skidelsky, 2006, p. 83).

This underlines their key disagreement: what are the best policies for safeguarding the liberal tradition? Keynes, in his letter to Hayek in response to *The Road to Serfdom* wondered: 'You admit here and there that there is a question of knowing where to draw the line... you give us no guidance whatever as to where to draw it [meaning on practical policy matters]' (Keynes, [1977] 2012, p. 386). This was the essence of the argument. Both believed in the principles of western liberalism and in individual choice. But, while Hayek was driven by abstract principle, Keynes was drawn by policy implementation. Hayek was concerned with the growing unchecked power of the state even in the Great Depression or during the heat of WWII. Keynes was always concerned with real situations and their immediate cures when discussing economic policy. Yet, it was his vision of employing whatever means necessary in order to effectively improve the economic conditions of the people that was to be the norm in policymaking in the 30 years that followed WWII. Hayek's belief in limited government, more unhindered market activity, would become very fashionable from the early 1980s and remains so up to the present. This intellectual conflict, emanating from pressing questions on monetary and fiscal policy during the Great Depression, brings into focus broader issues on the role and limits of markets in a liberal society. It is the breadth of vision that is inbuilt in the theoretical arguments of these two great economists that makes their views transcend their historical time and speak to us today with an immediacy that is both fresh and revealing.

3. Commentary and Notes on Further Reading

3.1 The Protagonists – A Brief Bibliography of Biographies

Robert Skidelsky opens his review of Wapshott's book by noting that 'there have been many books about Keynes and Hayek, but no one has written a book centred on their intellectual rivalry' (Skidelsky, 2013, p. 218)[6]. Professor Skidelsky is the best authority on

---

[6] Lawrence White's (2012) book was published the year after Wapshott's, and is, in many ways, a very different book. Its narrative style makes more extensive use of flashbacks to track the evolution of ideas, occasionally going back centuries. This shows how varied the narrative technique is between different contributions, and that

the subject as he is the author of the most celebrated intellectual biography of Keynes ever produced. His three volume work distinguishes three periods of Keynes's life and intellectual development. The first volume (Skidelsky, [1983] 1992) deals with his early life and ends with 1920, a year after Keynes published *The Economic Consequences of the Peace* (1919), a book that discredited the Versailles peace treaty and its harsh conditions for Germany. It is the book that propelled Keynes to stardom. The second volume (Skidelsky, [1992] 1994) deals with the period 1920-1937, and it is during this time that the rivalry with Hayek is the strongest, as this was a period when both economists are working on abstract macroeconomic theory. Finally, the third volume (Skidelsky, [2000] 2001) deals with the period 1937-1946 and finds Keynes engrossed in policy making. Keynes had to convince himself and others of when and how his theories were to apply. Most importantly Skidelsky's work shows that this intellectual battle with Hayek was one of many intellectual and policy battles running concurrently by Keynes in what was a full and varied life.

For those who find that three volumes spanning more than 1400 pages is a bit too much, there is a one volume edition running to about 850 pages (Skidelsky, 2004). There is also an extensive and rewarding review of the work in Harcourt and Turnell (2005) also found in Harcourt (2012). Skidelsky has written a short introduction on Keynes that is brief but goes into some detail on Keynes's work, making it possibly a challenging read for the non-economist (Skidelsky, 2010). A more accessible book on Keynes, written after the start of the recent financial crisis is Clarke (2009). Keynes, has never been in want of biographers, and there has been a fair number of biographies written since the early 1950s (Barnett, 2013; Davidson, [2007] 2009; Harrod, [1951] 1963; Hession, 1984; Moggridge, [1973] 1993 ; [1992] 1995). Biographies unavoidably carry the flavour of their times, as much as an impression of their subject, and there is some variation on how Keynes and his economics are portrayed. Finally, one can get an idea of Keynes's complex personality in a set of talks by celebrated historians of economic thought (Caldwell et al., 2009).

Hayek was born in 1899, 16 years after Keynes, and lived for another 46 years after Keynes's death in 1946. Alan Ebenstein published in 2001 the first full biography of Hayek, and introduced the following periodisation of Hayek's life: (1) 1899–1931. Hayek's early years in Vienna. (2) 1931–9. From Hayek's LSE appointment to 1939, when he was evacuated with the rest of the LSE to Cambridge. (3) 1939–1949. The war years and post-war period in England. (4) 1950–1962. In 1950 he moved to the University of Chicago, and remained in the USA until 1962. (5) 1962–1974. In 1962, Hayek returned to Germany and accepted a position in the University of Freiburg. (6) 1974–1992. In 1974

---

more work needs to be done on how narratives are constructed in history of economic thought books that are written for the public.

Hayek received the Nobel Prize in Economics. This marked his return to the public and academic spotlight. After 1974, his reputation as one of the greatest thinkers in economic and social theory would never really be in question. Furthermore, Hayek's complex evolution of thought is the subject of a number of intellectual biographies. The most important are: Caldwell (2004) which is written by the editor of Hayek's collected works, Ebenstein (2003) a work that complements Ebenstein's biography of Hayek, and Barry (1979) which was effectively the first book in this broad category, written when Hayek was still alive. Hayek (1994) is a detailed recounting of Hayek's life by himself through the use of a number of interviews with him.

What this periodisation shows is that the Keynes-Hayek intellectual battle found Hayek at the start of his long academic career, and Keynes at the end of his. Hayek not only outlived Keynes, but lived long enough to see in print a number of Keynes's biographies, reviewing the one written by Harrod (Hayek, 1952). He saw the publication of 30 volumes of Keynes's *Collected Writings* completed in the 1980s, and wrote a piece in *The Economist* on June 11, 1983 marking 100 years from Keynes's birth (Hayek, June 11, 1983), a milestone Keynes missed by 37 years.

Furthermore, the world had changed since Keynes's death. Hayek lived half his life after the Second World War, a period Keynes did not live to see. This also brings forth the realisation that our distance from these two actors and their lives is not proportional – nor is it so far removed in time that these differences do not matter. Hayek died less than 25 years ago, just after the fall of the Soviet Union, having seen the start of our current era and the end of the epoch that followed Keynes life.

3.2 Brief Notes on the Historiography of the 'Duel'

This naturally brings us to consider the context of their intellectual argument, and how our view of what happened in the 1930s has changed over time. A natural first step is to revisit the narrative of the 1930s constructed in the previous section and raise the following question: why and how was Hayek offered the Tooke Chair at the LSE, which set the stage to subsequent events? Recent findings by historian Susan Howson show that this dramatic duel was not the outcome of forethought. While it is true that the LSE was actively looking for an economic theorist to take up the Tooke Chair in Economic Science and Statistics in 1931, Howson shows that it was first offered to Jacob Viner (Howson, July 2012, pp. 15-6). However, Viner decided not to take it up. It was then offered to Hayek. Hayek's work until that time was all in German. His first book on business cycle theory was published in 1929, and Howson notes that it attracted the attention of Robbins (Howson, July 2012, p. 13). Robbins was probably instrumental in getting Hayek to give the set of lectures at the LSE on January 1931 that were published in book form (*Prices and Production*) and led to his LSE appointment. The episode is explored in detail in Howson (2011).

This is interesting because today it feels only natural that Hayek was at the LSE in the 1930s and that this battle was destined to happen. And while, it was, with hindsight, a very fortuitous appointment, the 1930s have not always been portrayed as the clash between these two intellectual giants. G.L.S. Shackle, who started his academic career in the 1930s, and was involved in the debates during this period, was the first to write a book about the intellectual discoveries of the 1920s and 1930s from a history of economic thought perspective (Shackle, 1967). His book, a classic in the field, is interesting to the modern reader for another reason as well. Hayek is effectively not mentioned in Shackle's story. *Prices and Production* does not even appear in the index. This omission was not picked up by reviewers of the book in academic journals at that time (see e.g. Baumol, 1968; Harrod, 1968). But most importantly it was in line with other books of the period on similar themes, like Donald Winch's study of the relation between Economics and Policy that included the interwar period (see Winch, 1969). This can be explained by remembering that in the late 1960s Keynes had won the day. But what is interesting is that the 1930s were not depicted as a clash between Hayek and Keynes, but as a clash between Keynes and a host of other economists and their theories, one of which, even if slightly more important than the others, was Hayek.

Since the 1990s narratives of this period, even when sympathetic to Keynes, would ascribe a larger role to Hayek. Laidler's modern classic on the Keynesian revolution has a chapter on the Austrian Theory of the Trade Cycle (see Laidler, 1999, pp. 27-50).[7] Robert Cord, who attempts to explain Keynes's success in the 1930s from a sociology of science perspective, places Hayek and his research program as the LSE competitor to Keynes and Cambridge (Cord, 2013). It can be argued that Hayek's relative importance in the 1930s debates, as viewed by the history of economic thought community, started to change in the 1980s, although there had been solitary voices making this argument much earlier with the most important being Hicks (1967). Marina Colonna, Harald Hagemann and Omar Hamouda the organisers of an important conference on Hayek's work in 1992, note 'while the conference and the essays are the consequence of the recent revival of interest in Hayek's work, several of them take up the ideas that engaged economists during the 1930s and early 1940s on Hayek's early work' (Colonna, Hagemann and Hamouda, 1994, XV). The two volume edition of the conference papers published in 1994 (Colonna and Hagemann, 1994; Colonna et al.,

---

[7] Laidler makes the following revealing remark 'Though there was no overt debate immediately after 1936 between "Mr Keynes and the Austrians" in the sense of an explicit exchange on the relative merits of these two systems, there surely was a silent debate in the minds of many economists as they decided which body of doctrine to adopt.' (Laidler, 1999, p. 49)

1994), re-invigorated interest in Hayek's early work, and changed how scholars viewed his early contributions.

Therefore, as the history of economic thought community started giving more attention to Hayek's early business cycle writings, the intellectual rivalry with Keynes also gained more prominence. The following example may be an indication of how much the narrative of the intellectual duel has captured the imagination of scholars in this community. Hayek never wrote a review of Keynes's *General Theory*. The reasons why this review never happened have been the subject of a number of academic papers (Caldwell, 1998; De Vecchi, 2006; Howson, 2001; Sans Bas, 2011). This research has been widely read and cited. As an indication, Caldwell's article has at least 14 articles and 6 books citing it today (July 2014). This shows how important this question has become for the history of economic thought community, as it is a missing piece in the narrative of Hayek's confrontation with Keynes in the 1930s. It also shows how historians create narratives, and focus on specific questions as these narratives gain prominence.

3.3 Modern Schools of Thought and Their Relation to Hayek's and Keynes's Writings

Between the 1940s and this revival of interest from the history of economic thought community, there was a community of scholars that continued working on Hayek's theoretical output and on Austrian business cycle theory. Hayek was not the only Austrian economist who emigrated to the USA, either before or soon after the Second World War. Many, most importantly Joseph Schumpeter, Gottfried von Haberler, Fritz Machlup, Oscar Morgenstern, and Ludwig von Mises, had accepted academic positions in the States in the first half of the 20th century. The story of this movement and the creation of a new Austrian school of thought in the USA is told in Vaughn ([1994] 1998). There is a substantial body of theoretical work that has been produced by these scholars and cannot be adequately surveyed here. A pointer of where to start may be to look at O'Driscoll and Rizzo ([1985] 1996), a seminal book on neo-Austrian economics, or possibly, Israel Kirzner's work (e.g. see Kirzner, [2000] 2006).

What should be noted, even briefly, is the work of macroeconomists within that school that trace their work back to Hayek's business cycle theory. Roger Garrison has been a major proponent, and has written extensively on the subject. Garrison (2001) gives a good overview of this material. Ebeling (1996) is an edited volume that is comprised of short essays on Austrian business cycle theory written for the general public. Garrison has two essays in that volume. The figure found in Ebeling (1996, p. 113) depicting the different types of Hayekian expansions was used in the explanation of Hayek's theory in the previous section. This also alludes to an important issue in approaching Hayek's and Keynes's work. Because the primary material is technical, conceptually difficult, and written primarily for academic economists, the general public often approaches this work through intermediaries.

Nevertheless, the difficulties of the key texts are not only a problem for the common reader. Therefore, interpretations of Hayek's work in the 1930s range between academic readers or even communities of academics viewing this material from different vantage points. One example is how history of economic thought scholars stress more the evolution of Hayek's thought focusing on issues of continuity and change in his research programme over his lifetime. A recent historical account of Hayek's research on business cycles can be found in Hansjoerg Klausinger's introduction in the relevant volumes of Hayek's collected works (Hayek, 2012a; 2012b). There Klausinger introduces a periodisation of Hayek's business cycle work, showing that it consists of different phases of analysis, as Hayek's understanding of equilibrium, expectations, capital and knowledge changed over his lifetime. This understanding would inevitably influence the simple narrative constructed in the previous section, as Hayek's analysis in *Prices and Production* is not his final word on the matter of business cycles, and that simplified depiction does not take into account important elements of Hayek's work on fixed capital, changing expectations, or more complex views of equilibrium.

On first reading, these issues may appear more like a sparring match between scholars interested in the minutiae of academic argument. I think this is not the case. Even questions concerning the core of Keynes's message have divided economists from the 1940s onwards. Today, economists that self-identify as Keynesians might disagree on almost anything from policy issues to philosophical and methodological questions, or even what constitutes proper economic analysis and what does not. What unites them is a belief that the market economy is flawed in some way, and that the government has a role to play especially in periods of economic crisis. Then diverse schools of thought see Keynes's original texts as part of their intellectual heritage or ascribe a symbolic value to his work. The most dominant school in academic economics today that follows this line is the New Keynesians, who identify market imperfections, especially issues of price stickiness, or information imperfections, as key reasons why the market system operates less than perfectly. This field's output is quite technical and good introductions for the non-specialist are not easy to find. A suggestion is Gali (2008) especially the introduction and concluding chapters that are non-technical and broad in scope.

Keynes's writings are more central and revisited regularly in theory discussions by another school of thought, the post-Keynesians. This is a very diverse school, with many strands focusing on different analytical and methodological approaches. An introduction to this literature can be found in Lavoie ([2007 [2009]) or Harcourt (2006). An example may give an indication of how much the interpretation of Keynes's message varies between these two traditions. Paul Davidson, an important American Post-Keynesian, finds fundamental uncertainty to be the key insight of Keynes. He sees the future as unknowable, and disagrees with efforts to quantify this uncertainty by placing probability estimates on possible future outcomes. This leads Davidson to a completely different analytical understanding of the economy to that of the New Keynesians, whose models use expected values and probability outcomes.

This means that the challenges faced when popularising Keynes's fundamental insights are not equivalent with those of a physicist trying to make Einstein's theory of relativity broadly understood by the general public. Different physicists may vary in how they decide to represent Einstein's pioneering theory but would not be in intellectual disagreement on what Einstein's theory is about. With economists that identify as Keynesians the intellectual disagreements are much deeper. Therefore, one could even argue that 'Keynesian economist' as a term has become a conventional label for a large group of economists who occupy similar positions in the political spectrum, and this is their only uniting thread. This means that any reader interested in Keynes and his theoretical work must be aware how varied these traditions are, in order to avoid confusion between the different claims on Keynes's message.

Hayek's relation to macroeconomic theory after the 1940s faces different problems to Keynes's. Whereas Keynes had a diverse following, Hayek's technical work had, after the 1940s, almost no following outside the new Austrians. He may have been in the University of Chicago in the 1950s and early 1960s, but this does not mean he effectively influenced macroeconomic thought there, or that his technical work was seen as a progenitor to that school of thought. Skousen (2005) has written an accessible book on the relation between the Austrians and the Chicago school of economics.

Furthermore, some scholars have argued that New Classical macroeconomic theory, starting from the late 1970s and early 1980s, and focusing on general equilibrium business cycle analysis with a capital theory component, is really a continuation of Hayek's research work. Ruhl (1994) and more extensively Zijp (1992) assess this thesis. They find this not to be the case, as Hayek's work has only a superficial resemblance to the literature of dynamic stochastic general equilibrium models as it unfolded from the 1980s onwards. This shows that both Hayek's and Keynes's technical work on business cycles is not a linear progenitor of later 'clashes' between e.g. post war American mainstream Keynesians and Monetarists, or the modern publicised divide between 'freshwater' and 'saltwater' economics. The only thread in any such narrative that connects these debates is that the two sides occupy different policy positions, with each side providing arguments for and against government intervention in the economy.

The question that naturally arises as we look back in this discussion and wonder: why set up a narrative around Hayek and Keynes? Hayek lived until 1992 but his technical economic work was neglected after the 1940s, and Keynes died in 1946 and his economics lived on but in the hands of other theorists. Their clash in the 1930s is important from a history of economic thought perspective, but so are other clashes or disagreements back then, for example, between Keynes and Tinbergen (another Nobel laureate in economics). Why has this debate gained such momentum with the general public?

3.4 The Broader Picture

The answer to this question is that both theorists have become standard bearers of very broad policy positions. Their work was deep, insightful and varied as it combined economic analysis with broader visions of the social order. Keynes's diverse literary output became the inspiration in later generations of economists for developing a more complicated view of how capitalism works and why it occasionally needs a visible hand to take action when invisible ones fail. In order to really understand the scope of Keynes's vision, and also see his brilliance as an essayist, it is important to visit the primary texts and decide on the merits of his arguments first hand.

Keynes's Collected Writings ([1971-1989] 2012) have been published by Macmillan for the Royal Economic Society. They comprise of 30 volumes in total, edited by Donald Moggridge, Austin Robinson and Elizabeth Johnson. From 2012, all of them are available in paperback. The first ten volumes are Keynes's published books with *The General Theory* being volume 7. Volumes 13, 14 and 29 deal with the period prior to and after the publication of *The General Theory*, and give interesting information of how the ideas it contains came into existence. The other volumes deal with Keynes's varied activities and correspondence.

Hayek, viewed crassly as the other policy pole in this free market vs. government intervention narrative, has a complex position in relation to the role and limits of government action. In oversimplified accounts, like the one attempted in the previous section, the usual interpretation put forward is that all government action is problematic and unwelcomed. However, Hayek had a much more refined theoretical position that emanated from his understanding of the western liberal tradition. He wrote extensively on the importance of the rule of law in demarcating the limits of policy action. That is why, in *The Constitution of Liberty,* he notes that 'freedom of economic activity has meant freedom under the law, not the absence of all government action' (Hayek, 2011, p. 329). And adds, several pages later, 'in other words, it is the character rather that the volume of government activity that is important' (Hayek, 2011, p. 331). He goes on to argue that a government that is not very active but, when it acts its actions negate the rule of law, can do much more harm than a government 'more concerned with economic affairs' that respects, however, societal rules that demarcate what it can and cannot do.

The above brief vignette cannot do justice to Hayek's argument, and this is why there is good reason to approach his writings directly and read *The Constitution of Liberty* first hand, if one is concerned about the proper limits of government action in a liberal democracy. All of Hayek's writings are in the process of being published in one series as his collected works, by the University of Chicago Press. The general editor is Bruce Caldwell. The first ten volumes (Hayek, 1988; 1991; 1992; 1995; 1997; 1999a; 1999b; 2007b; 2012a; 2012b) plus volumes 12 (Hayek, 2007a), 13 (Hayek, 2010), 15 (Hayek, 2014) and 17 (Hayek, 2011) are out. In total, 19 volumes are expected to form Hayek's works. These works have extensive introductions from leading scholars in the field. Hayek (1995) deals with the Hayek-Keynes 'clash' and reprints the relevant material from the 1930s with an introduction by Caldwell. It should be read in conjunction with Hayek's work on business cycles and money which occupy volumes 5–8 (Hayek, 1999a; 1999b; 2012a; 2012b). Finally, the rest of the volumes republish important texts by Hayek in philosophy, politics, social theory and the history of economic thought and show the breadth of his contributions in all these fields.

4. Concluding Remarks

Economics is a subject that the common reader finds interesting and important for good reason. At the same time, much academic research is in a form that is not accessible to the public. This is because it has developed its own terminology, machinery and form of exposition that the non-specialist finds difficult to penetrate. And yet the common reader, in his demand for literature that fills this gap, has focused on something that is occasionally lost in academic study. This is the sharp focus of a grand narrative that inevitably glosses over detail and technical argument, but tries to capture the undercurrents that shape our economic and social reality. This, I believe, explains the fascination and popularity of the Keynes vs. Hayek intellectual debate. The question that remains is whether exercises like the one attempted in this paper can add to the reader's experience, without alienating him, or making on him unreasonable demands.

By dividing up the texts into a narrative, conventionally constructed, and a discussion, which acts both as a bookshelf, and as a second voice, the reader is immediately introduced to multiple viewpoints. This second voice, a commentary on a narrative, adds detail, but also problematises part of the narrative. This, I think, is this scheme's greatest strength. It does not let the reader leave the narrative satisfied that he knows all that there is to know of substance on this topic. It does not hide away in footnotes, endnotes or bibliographies this second text, but brings it forward signalling to the reader its importance.

The reader is invited not only to read these two texts, but also to start exploring the references so that he can decide on these matters by himself. Inevitably, this exercise is successful when the reader, after a journey through primary and other texts, finds the simplicity and crassness of the first narrative close to offensive. At best he may come to agree with Robbins who, in the reading list he gave to students of his history of economic thought class, noted: 'books about books are chiefly useful for those who know the books they are about' (Robbins, 2000, p. 337).

There are many questions to be answered in relation to how we apply this scheme in practice. For the Keynes vs. Hayek case study attempted above, I will concentrate on the following three areas: (1) the selection and presentation of further reading, (2) the different ways by which the commentary 'crosses paths' with the narrative and, (3) what does this narrative and commentary tell us about its targeted 'common reader'.

Starting with pointers for further reading, it should be clarified that not all texts referred to in the commentary are there to fulfil this function. The various subsections of the commentary have different purposes, only one of which is to provide further reading the reader should look up. With references where this is the main purpose, some brief comments are given on what this reading has to offer. For example, in the section of the biographies of Keynes and Hayek, Skidelsky's three volume biography is mentioned first, simply because it is the standard upon which all biographies of Keynes are judged, and because it presents us with a useful periodisation of Keynes's life. But then alternatives are offered which are more concise and therefore reasonable suggestions, like Skidelsky's introduction to Keynes or Clarke's book. Furthermore, the references given for further reading must be material that the public would have reasonably easy access to. This is why I avoided references to subscription journals, as the reader is not part of the academic community or necessarily affiliated with an academic institution. Books come at a cost, but are available in bookshops, and can be bought by the reader depending on what he wants to read more about – Keynes, Hayek, modern Keynesian theory or neo-Austrian theory etc.

A possible criticism of the section is that the referencing still has an academic flavour. Little use has been made of material freely available on the internet, or other forms of information transition, as it makes references only to other texts. There is, however, substantial audio-visual material on Hayek, who gave recorded interviews and talks during his lifetime. Also there are online resources by scholars writing blog entries or discussing this intellectual battle on videos available online.[8] How to integrate these resources is not a simple question, but there are ways to be more imaginative. A possible example is a Prezi titled The F. A. Hayek Global Tracker, created by G. Ransom, with free online access,[9] which plots Hayek's travels through his life with playable videos on each stop taken from Hayek's interviews. There remains, therefore, substantial scope for

---

[8] For example: http://www.youtube.com/watch?v=PLBOKq4On7k (accessed on 06/07/2014)
[9] You can find it at: http://prezi.com/v2k0vacx7huf/the-f-a-hayek-global-tracker/ (accessed 05/07/2014)

improvement on how to make resources available to readers and entice them into exploring further the subject.

For the reader to take this step she needs to realise the limits of the narrative she has just read. This is one of the reasons for having the commentary structured separately, so that it is free standing and on equal ground with the main narrative. In this case study the commentary took up both factual points of the narrative, for example clarifying how Hayek got the position in the LSE, and broader theoretical points, for example noting Hayek's complex position on the rule of law and government action. Furthermore, it questioned the viewpoint of the scholar-populariser, by explaining how different academic economists have varying interpretations of Keynes's and Hayek's theories. But the commentary went further than that. It problematised the basic structure of the narrative by discussing its historiography and the links these theorists have with contemporary schools of economic thought. Therefore, the reader was given clear signals on the limits of this narrative structure, so that she does not leave the discussion with a distorted view of economics in the 20th century, or Hayek's and Keynes's role in its development.

How effective the commentary is in conveying all this information to its prospective reader is open to discussion. Part of the answer lies on the other side of the coin, the reader herself. It is unreasonable to assume that all general readers, whatever their background, will come to the same common understanding after reading through this article. Inevitably, the audience for which most things will fall in place by the time they have finished reading is much narrower, and the implicit demands of the text already gives us an indication of its constitution. The use of supply and demand curves in section two shows us that the reader will have some basic knowledge of economics, which may be no more than a semester or so in higher education, but enough to make her comfortable with this abstraction.[10] This points to the following definition of the 'modern common reader' articulated by Frank Kermode: 'the person [who] has attended a university and studied with accomplished scholars, but then has gone out into the professional world to make a living' (Knight, 2003, p. 154). This is, to use, again, Kermode's words – out of context – 'an "elite minority", clearly differentiated from the uneducated on the one hand and the specialists on the other. In fact, it was Johnson's Common Reader' (Kermode, 1983, p. 3). This is, in some ways, no surprise. The majority of humanity is not interested in the Hayek-Keynes debate, even in the five minute rap version, and those who are interested enough to read a book, or at least an article, are a very small minority.

---

[10] I would like to thank Nuno Martins for pointing this out.

Even if we agree that this is our target audience[11] there is still the fear that the commentary becomes too heavy and technical so that the reader finds herself again to be an outsider. In some ways it can be argued that the commentary constructed in section three was too ambitious in detail and referencing. It created its own subtext making it demanding reading to even this audience. Therefore, it simply shifted the problem from the main narrative to the commentary. This is, to some degree, unavoidable, as it is part of what the commentary is expected to do, which is to unearth questions silenced in the narrative and upset its simplified 'truths'. This means that the commentary, like the narrative, has as its objective to inform, or to use a more old fashioned term, to educate its readers.

Therefore we return to the core question, which is whether these popularisations have an educational element or are here simply to entertain. If the point is only to entertain, then the dramatis personae are essentially irrelevant. The author may construct a gripping story around the clash of Hayek vs. Keynes, or Gore Vidal vs. Truman Capote, or even Paris Hilton vs. Kim Kardashian. These all have the ability to entertain. However, I do think that by choosing Hayek vs. Keynes the public is looking for something more. We ought to respect this wish. And we must find ways to address it appropriately.

Acknowledgements

I would like to thank B. Caldwell, J. Forder, G.C. Harcourt, H. Klausinger, N. Martins, G. Meeks and S. Egashira for valuable feedback. I would also like to thank the participants of the relevant session in the ESHET 2014 conference in Lausanne.

References

Altick, R.D. [1957] (1998) *The English Common Reader*. Columbus, Ohio State University Press

Aydinonat, N.E. (2012) 'The two images of economics: why the fun disappears when difficult questions are at stake?'. *Journal of Economic Methodology,* vol. 19, no. 3, 243-58.

---

[11] And there are many publishers who would beg to disagree. Therefore, issues of marketability and gross sales would be part to any such discussion between authors, their publishers and their targeted reader. In this there have been critical voices, with Frank Kermode writing 'The Common Reader is of course not a person but a constituency, and everybody not seeking to grind an axe must know that by now it is a pretty rotten borough' (Kermode, 1983, 3). The core question is what does this constituency want? To call it a rotten borough implying that what it wants is what is on offer and currently consumed, is to take too neoclassical a stand on the matter for my taste.

Backhouse, R.E. (2012) 'Economics is a difficult and serious subject'. *Journal of Economic Methodology,* vol. 19, no. 3, 231-41.

Barnett, V. (2013) *John Maynard Keynes*. London, Routledge.

Barry, N.P. (1979) *Hayek's Social and Economic Philosophy*. London, Macmillan.

Baumol, W.J. (1968) 'Book review of *The Years of High Theory: Inventions and Tradition in Economic Thought 1926-1939*. By G.L.S. Shackle.' *The American Economic Review,* vol. 58, no. 3, 565-566.

Burgin, A. (2012) *The Great Persuasion. Reinventing Free Markets since the Depression*. Cambridge, Harvard University Press.

Caldwell, B. (1998) 'Why didn't Hayek review Keynes's *General Theory*?'. *History of Political Economy,* vol. 30, no. 4, 545-69.

Caldwell, B. (2004) *Hayek's Challenge*. Chicago, University of Chicago Press.

Caldwell, B., C. Goodwin, K.D. Hoover & E.R. Weintraub. (2009) John Maynard Keynes of Bloomsbury: Four Short Talks. *Economic Research Initiatives at Duke (ERID) Research Paper No. 23* available at: http://ssrn.com/abstract=1348679.

Clarke, P. 4 February 2012. 'Keynes - Hayek by Nicholas Wapshott.' *The Guardian,* Guardian review, 9.

Clarke, P. (2009) *Keynes. The Twentieth Century's Most Influential Economist*. London, Bloomsbury.

Cochran, J.P. (2011) 'Keynes Hayek: The Clash that Defined Modern Economics by Nicholas Wapshott'. *Quarterly Journal of Austrian Economics,* vol. 14 no. 4, 474-9.

Colonna, M. & Hagemann, H. (1994) *Money and Business Cycles*. Aldershot, Edward Elgar.

Colonna, M., H. Hagemann & O. Hamouda. (1994) *Capitalism, Socialism and Knowledge*. Aldershot, Edward Elgar.

Congdon, T. 29 February (2012) 'How Keynes overwhelmed Hayek'. *Times Literary Supplement.*

Cord, R. (2013) *Reinterpreting the Keynesian Revolution*. London, Routledge.

Cornish, S. (2013) 'The Hayek Literature: Nicholas Wapshott's *Keynes Hayek: The Clash that Defined Modern Economics*', in *Hayek A Colaborative Biography. Part I Influences from Mises to Bartley,* ed. R. Leeson, 74-79. London, Macmillan.

Davidson, P. [2007] (2009) *John Maynard Keynes*. Basingstoke Palgrave Macmillan

Davidson, S. (2012) 'Keynes Hayek: The Clash that Defined Modern Economics By Nicholas Wapshott'. *Policy,* vol. 28, no. 2, 63-4.

De Vecchi, N. (2006) 'Hayek and the General Theory'. *The European Journal of the History of Economic Thought,* vol. 13, no. 2, 233-58.

Ebeling, R.M. (1996) *The Austrian Theory of the Trade Cycle*. Auburn, Alabama, Ludwig Von Mises Institute.

Ebenstein, A. (2001) *Friedrich Hayek. A Biography*. New York, Palgrave.

Ebenstein, A. (2003) *Hayek's Journey*. New York, Macmillan.

Fleury, J.B. (2012) 'The Evolving notion of Relevance: An historical perspective of the "economics made fun" movement'. *Journal of Economic Methodology,* vol. 19, no. 3, 303-16.

Gali, J. (2008) *Monetary Policy, Inflation, and the Business Cycle: An Introduction to the New Keynesian Framework*. Princeton, Princeton University Press.

Garrison, R.W. (2001) *Time and Money*. London, Routledge.

Harcourt, G.C. (2006) *The Structure of Post-Keynesian Economics*. Cambridge, CUP.

Harcourt, G.C. (2012) *On Skidelsky's Keynes and Other Essays: Selected Essays of G. C. Harcourt* London, Palgrave Macmillan.

Harcourt, G.C. & S. Turnell. (2005) 'On Skidelsky's Keynes'. *Economic and Political Weekly,* vol. 40, no. 47, 4931-4946.

Harrod, R. [1951] (1963) *The Life of John Maynard Keynes*. London, Macmillan.

Harrod, R.F. (1968) 'Book review of The Years of High Theory. Invention and Tradition in Economic Thought 1926-1939. By G.L.S. Shackle'. *The Economic Journal,* vol. 78, no. 311, 660-664.

Hayek, F.A. (1944) *The Road to Serfdom*. London.

Hayek, F.A. (1952) 'Review of Harrod's *Life of J.M. Keynes*'. *The Journal of Modern History,* vol. 24, no. 2, 195-8.

Hayek, F.A. (1988) *The Fatal Conceit: The Errors of Socialism. Volume 1 of the Collected Works of F.A. Hayek*. Chicago, Chicago University Press.

Hayek, F.A. (1991) *The Trend of Economic Thinking. Volume 3 of the Collected Works of F.A. Hayek*. Chicago, Chicago University Press.

Hayek, F.A. (1992) *The Fortunes of Liberalism. Volume 4 of the Collected Works of F.A. Hayek*. Chicago, Chicago University Press.

Hayek, F.A. (1994) *Hayek on Hayek*. London, Routledge.

Hayek, F.A. (1995) *Contra Keynes and Cambridge. Volume 9 of the Collected Works of F.A. Hayek*. Chicago, Chicago University Press.

Hayek, F.A. (1997) *Socialism and War. Volume 10 of the Collected Works of F.A. Hayek.* Chicago, Chicago University Press.

Hayek, F.A. (1999a) *Good Money. Part I. Volume 5 of the Collected Works of F.A. Hayek.* Chicago, Chicago University Press.

Hayek, F.A. (1999b) *Good Money. Part II. Volume 6 of the Collected Works of F.A. Hayek.* Chicago, Chicago University Press.

Hayek, F.A. (2007a) *The Pure Theory of Capital. Volume 12 of the Collected Works of F.A. Hayek.* Chicago, Chicago University Press.

Hayek, F.A. (2007b) *The Road to Serfdom. Volume 2 of the Collected Works of F.A. Hayek.* Chicago, Chicago University Press.

Hayek, F.A. (2010) *Studies on the Abuse and Decline of Reason. Volume 13 of the Collected Works of F.A. Hayek.* Chicago, Chicago University Press.

Hayek, F.A. (2011) *The constitution of Liberty. The Definitive Edition. Volume 17 of the Collected Works of F.A. Hayek.* Chicago, Chicago University Press.

Hayek, F.A. (2012a) *Business Cycles. Part I. Volume 7 of the Collected Works of F.A. Hayek.* Chicago, Chicago University Press.

Hayek, F.A. (2012b) *Business Cycles. Part II. Volume 8 of the Collected Works of F.A. Hayek.* Chicago, Chicago University Press.

Hayek, F.A. (2014) *The Market and Other Orders. Volume 15 of The Collected Works of F.A. Hayek.* Chicago, University of Chicago Press

Hayek, F.A. [1931] (1935) *Prices and Production.* London, Routledge.

Hayek, F.A. June 11, (1983) 'The Keynes Centenary: The Austrian Critique'. *The Economist*, 45-8.

Hession, C. (1984) *John Maynard Keynes: a personal biography of the man who revolutionized capitalism and the way we live.* New York, Macmillan.

Hicks, J. (1967) 'The Hayek Story', in *Critical Essays in Monetary Theory.* Oxford, Clarendon Press.

Hoover, K.R. (2003) *Economics as ideology : Keynes, Laski, Hayek, and the creation of contemporary politics.* Oxford, Rowman & Littlefield

Howson, S. (2001) 'Why Didn't Hayek Review Keynes's General Theory? A Partial Answer'. *History of Political Economy,* vol. 33, no. 2, 369-374.

Howson, S. (2011) *Lionel Robbins.* Cambridge, CUP.

Howson, S. July 2012. 'The Uses of Biography and the History of Economics', in *25th Jubilee conference of the History of Economic Thought Society of Australia.* Melbourn.

Johnson, S. (1866) *Lives of English Poets Vol. II.* Philadelphia J.B. Lippincott & Co.

Jones, D.S. (2012) *Masters of the Universe: Hayek, Friedman, and the Birth of Neoliberal Politics* Princeton, New Jersey, Princeton University Press.

Kermode, F. (1983) 'The Common Reader'. *Daedalus,* vol. 112, no. 1, 1-11.

Keynes, J.M. (1919) *The economic consequences of the peace.* London, Macmillan

Keynes, J.M. (1926) *The End of Laissez-faire.* London, The Hogarth Press

Keynes, J.M. [1936] (1973)*The General Theory of Employment, Interest, and Money. Volume VII of The Collected Writings of John Maynard Keynes.* London, Macmillan.

Keynes, J.M. [1971-1989] 2012. *The Collected Writings of John Maynard Keynes. 30 Volumes.* London, Macmillan.

Keynes, J.M. [1977] (2012) *The Collected Writings of John Maynard Keynes: Volume XVII.* London, Macmillan (reprint of 2012 Cambridge University Press).

Keynes, J.M. [1982] (2012) *Activities 1931-1939: World Crises and Policies in Britain and America. Volume XXI of the Collected Writings of John Maynard Keynes.* London, Macmillan (reprinted by Cambridge University Press in paperback)

Kirzner, I.M. [2000] (2006) *The Driving Force of the Market: Essays in Austrian Economics.* Abingdon, Routledge.

Knight, C.J. (2003) *Uncommon Readers. Denis Donoghue, Frank Kermode, George Steiner, and the Tradition of the Common Reader.* Toronto, University of Toronto Press.

Koehn, N.F. 23 October 2011. 'The Tale of the Dueling Economists'. *The New York Times (New York edition),* BU 8.

Laidler, D. (1999) *Fabricating the Keynesian Revolution.* Cambridge, Cambridge University Press.

Lamm, D.S. (1993) 'Economics and the common reader', in *The Spread of Economic Ideas,* eds. D. Colander & A.W. Coats, 95-109. Cambridge, CUP.

Lavoie, M. [2007 [2009]. *Introduction to Post-Keynesian Economics.* Basingstoke, Palgrave Macmillan.

Maki, U. (2012) 'On the philosophy of the new kiosk economics of everything'. *Journal of Economic Methodology,* vol. 19, no. 3, 219-30.

Moggridge, D. [1973] (1993) *Keynes.* London, Fontana/Collins.

Moggridge, D. [1992] (1995) *Maynard Keynes: An Economists Biography.* London, Routledge.

O'Driscoll, G.P. & M.J. Rizzo. [1985] (1996) *The Economics of Time and Ignorance.* London, Routledge.

Patrick, M. (2012) 'Nicholas Wapshott, Keynes Hayek: The Clash That Defined Modern Economics'. *Journal of Value Inquiry,* vol. 46, no. 1, 97-102.

Repapis, C. (2013) 'The scholar as reader: the last 50 years of economic theory seen through G.C. Harcourt's book reviews'. *Cambridge Journal of Economics*, doi: 10.1093/cje/bes082.

Robbins, L. (1934) *The Great Depression*. New York, Macmillan.

Robbins, L. (2000) *A History of Economic Thought*. Princeton, Princeton University Press.

Ross, J. (2010) *The Intellectual Life of the British Working Classes*. New Haven, Yale University Press.

Ruhl, C. (1994) 'The Transformation of business cycle theory: Hayek, Lucas and a change in the notion of equilibrium', in *Money and Business Cycles,* eds. M. Colonna & H. Hagemann. Aldershot, Edward Elgar.

Sans Bas, D. (2011) 'Hayek's Critique of The General Theory: a New View of the Debate between Hayek and Keynes'. *The Quarterly Journal of Austrian Economics,* vol. 14, no. 3, 288-310.

Shackle, G.L.S. (1967) *The Years of High Theory. Invention and Tradition in Economic Thought 1926-1939*. London, Cambridge University Press.

Skidelsky, R. (2004) *John Maynard Keynes 1883-1946 : economist, philosopher, statesman*. London, Macmillan.

Skidelsky, R. (2006) 'Hayek versus Keynes: The road to reconciliation', in *The Cambridge Companion to Hayek,* ed. E. Feser. Cambridge, Cambridge University Press.

Skidelsky, R. (2010) *Keynes: A Very Short Introduction*. Oxford, Oxford University Press.

Skidelsky, R. (2013) 'Book review of *Keynes Hayek: The Clash that Defined Modern Economics'*. By Nicholas Wapshott. *Historian,* vol. 75, no. 1, 218-9.

Skidelsky, R. [1983] (1992) *John Maynard Keynes : Hopes Betrayed 1883-1920* London, Macmillan

Skidelsky, R. [1992] (1994) *John Maynard Keynes : The economist as Saviour 1920-1937*. London, Macmillan.

Skidelsky, R. [2000] (2001) *John Maynard Keynes: Fighting for Britain 1937-1946*. London, Macmillan.

Skousen, M. (2005) *Vienna and Chicago. Friends or Foes?* Washington DC, Capital Press.

Steele, G.R. (2012) 'Book review of *Keynes Hayek: The Clash That Defined Modern Economics* by Nicholas Wapshott'. *Economic Affairs,* vol. 32, no. 3, 118-9.

Tankersley, W. (2012) 'Clash of the Economic Titans'. *Public Administration Review,* vol. 72, no. 3, 469-471.

Vaughn, K.I. [1994] (1998) *Austrian Economics in America*. Cambridge, CUP.

Vromen, J.J. (2009) 'The booming economics-made-fun genre: more than having fun, but less than economic imperialism'. *Erasmus Journal for Philosophy and Economics,* vol. 2, no. 1, 70-99.

Wapshott, N. (2011) *Keynes Hayek: The Clash That Defined Modern Economics.* New York, W.W. Norton and Company.

Webb, R.K. (1955) *The British Working Class Reader 1970-1848.* London, George Aleen and Unwin.

White, L.H. (2012) *The Clash of Economic Ideas.* Cambridge, Cambridge University Press.

Winch, D. (1969) *Economics and Policy. A Historical Study.* London, Hodder and Stoughton.

Yergin, D. & J. Stanislaw. (2002) *The Commanding Heights: The Battle for the World Economy.* London, Simon & Schuster.

Zijp, R. (1992) *Austrian and New Classical,Business Cycle Theories.* Amsterdam, Thesis Publishers.

SUGGESTED CITATION:

Repapis, C. (2014) 'J.M. Keynes, F.A. Hayek and the Common Reader'. *Economic Thought*, 3.2, pp. 1-20.
http://www.worldeconomicsassociation.org/files/journals/economicthought/WEA-ET-3-2-Repapis.pdf

Reconciling Ricardo's Comparative Advantage with Smith's Productivity Theory

Jorge Morales Meoqui[1], Independent Researcher
jorgemorales3@gmail.com

Abstract

There are three main claims in the paper: first, there is sufficient evidence for affirming that Ricardo adhered to Smith's productivity theory; second, Ricardo's original demonstration of the comparative-advantage proposition is indeed compatible and complementary with respect to the latter; and third, Ricardo agreed with Smith's multifactorial explanation of the pattern of trade, which includes increasing returns and economies of scale. These results suggest that the level of compatibility between the international trade theories of Smith and Ricardo is significantly higher than it is currently reflected in the economic literature. They also add a new perspective to the ongoing process of reassessment of Smith's contributions to international trade theory, further strengthening the view that he was indeed an outstanding international trade theorist.

Keywords: comparative advantage, David Ricardo, Adam Smith, international trade theory, division of labour, free trade

JEL-Codes: B12; F10

---

2. Introduction

> 'The end of all commerce is to increase production.' David Ricardo, *Principles* (1817)

Throughout the 19th century economists relied mostly upon Adam Smith's celebrated book *An Inquiry into the Nature and Causes of the Wealth of Nations* ([1776] 1976) for praising the benefits of specialisation and free trade. For the most part of the 20th century, however, the perception prevailed that Smith was not an outstanding international trade theorist because he allegedly failed to discover the 'law' of comparative advantage.[2]

---

[1] Homepage: http://wuvienna.academia.edu/JorgeMoralesMeoqui
[2] The list of those who have criticized Smith for not discovering the 'law' of comparative advantage is actually too long to mention here. Some of these critics, however, also acknowledge and appreciate Smith's positive

Since the neoclassical theory of static comparative advantage was generally regarded as the high-point of free trade thinking (Viner, 1937, p. 104), all the other contributions to international trade theory had to be evaluated in terms of how close they came to the comparative-advantage statement (Elmslie and James, 1993). According to this yardstick, Smith's insights on international trade seem to be obsolete.

In the late 1970s Smith's contributions to international trade theory started to receive more attention and appreciation.[3] This process gained considerably more steam during the 1980s with the formulation of the so called *New Trade Theory*, in which traditional trade models based on the neoclassical theory of static comparative advantage were supplemented by new trade models emphasising increasing returns and technical progress. The demand for these new trade models originated from the fact that the traditional neoclassical models of static comparative advantage were inadequate for explaining the real-world trade pattern in those years, which was predominantly intra-industry-trade (Krugman, 1993; 2009).

The proponents of the New Trade Theory pioneered some novel modelling techniques, but the aspects they were trying to emphasise in their trade models were not new at all. They were already present in Smith's explanation of the benefits of international trade in the *Wealth of Nations*.[4] This led to the current perception that Smith was a much better international trade theorist than he had previously been given credit for (Elmslie and James, 1993, p. 72).

Notwithstanding this remarkable comeback, the last remaining stumbling block towards Smith's complete rehabilitation as an international trade theorist is still in place: the critique that he failed to discover the 'law' of comparative advantage as defined by the neoclassical theory of international trade. Furthermore, the greater emphasis on increasing returns has widened the perceived rift between Smith's contributions to international trade theory and the static view of comparative advantage attributed to fellow classical political economist David Ricardo. Some scholars have even gone as far as to affirm that Smith and Ricardo had opposing logics of trade.[5]

---

contributions to international trade theory. Bloomfield (1994 [1975], p. 111), for example, states: 'Admittedly, Smith was not a great trade theorist, but he comes up, on the whole, with a performance that deserves respectful consideration.' See also Mynt (1977), Kurz (1992) and Blecker (1997). For a brief overview of other prominent critics of Smith, see Bloomfield (1994, pp. 109-110).

[3] See West (1978).

[4] The Smithean origins of the *New Trade Theory* have been highlighted by several authors, for example West (1990), Elmslie and James (1993), Kurz (1997) and Kibritcioglu (2002). It is also recognised by at least one of the leading proponents of the *New Trade Theory* (Krugman, 1990). For the relationship between the division of labour and technological progress see Elmslie (1994b).

[5] See Buchanan and Yoon (2002). Russ Roberts has recently echoed the notion about Smith's and Ricardo's distinct and opposing logics of trade in his popular podcast EconTalk (http://www.econtalk.org/archives/2010/02/roberts_on_smit.html).

This may lead to a greater divulgence of this notion among current economics students, which are presumably the largest group of subscribers to Roberts' podcast.

Prior research efforts have been headed towards discovering some traces of comparative advantage in the *Wealth of Nations* (Elmslie and James, 1993; Elmslie, 1994a) and re-evaluating the role of absolute advantage so that it is not perceived merely as a flawed antecedent of comparative advantage (Blecker, 1997). A more or less common theme of these efforts has been the view that in order to achieve the goal of completely rehabilitating Smith as an outstanding international trade theorist, one has to bring his insights on international trade somehow closer to the comparative-advantage proposition. The present paper will show that the same goal can be accomplished more easily by reintegrating the latter to Smith's framework.

Fortunately, all the necessary pieces for accomplishing the task are already in place. The point of departure is the accurate interpretation of the four numbers in the famous numerical demonstration of comparative advantage in Ricardo's book *On the Principles of Political Economy and Taxation* ([1817] 2004). As Ruffin (2002; 2005) has shown, they should be interpreted as the number of men working for a year required to produce *some unspecified amounts* of wine and cloth traded between England and Portugal.[6] The correct interpretation of the numerical example has led to a better understanding of its original purpose. As I have argued in a previous paper (Morales Meoqui, 2011), the main purpose of the numerical example was to prove the new proposition that the labour theory of value does not regulate the relative value of commodities in international trade when the factors of production are immobile between countries. Ricardo then mentioned the associated corollary regarding comparative advantage, i.e. that a country might import a certain amount of a commodity although it can produce these commodities internally with less amount of labour time than the exporting country.

Based on the above interpretation of the numerical example in the *Principles*, the present paper refutes the notion that Ricardo considered his original proof of the comparative-advantage proposition as an alternative explanation of the origin and benefits of trade. On the contrary, Ricardo repeatedly stated his agreement with Smith's famous proposition that the extension of the market provided by foreign trade would lead to productivity gains at home. Furthermore, the paper also refutes the notion that Ricardo offered an alternative explanation for international trade patterns by showing that he actually agreed with Smith's multifactorial explanation of the pattern of trade.

The first section of the paper outlines the two alternative explanations of the origin and benefits of international trade and rejects the attribution of the constant-labour-

---

[6] Sraffa (1930, p. 541) interpreted Ricardo's numbers as the number of men whose labour is required for one year in order to produce a given quantity of cloth and wine. Ruffin pointed out in a personal communication with me that Sraffa's interpretation was correct but incomplete since it did not say that Ricardo's numbers were the amounts of labour contained in the amounts of cloth and wine traded. Ruffin's interpretation has rapidly gained supporters – Maneschi (2004, 2008), Aldrich (2004) and Morales Meoqui (2011) and Rassekh (2012).

costs assumption to Ricardo. The second section is dedicated to proving that Ricardo actually adhered to Smith's productivity theory. The third section identifies the relevant cost comparison for specialisation and trade. The fourth section argues that Ricardo agreed with Smith's multifactorial explanation of international trade patterns, which includes increasing returns and economies of scale. The last section before the conclusions outlines what all of this means for the reassessment of Smith's contributions to international trade theory.

3. Two Explanations Regarding the Origin and Benefits of Trade

As Smith explains in the *Wealth of Nations*, the division of labour plays a pivotal role in increasing the wealth of individuals as well as nations.[7] Individuals specialise and trade with each other within and between national borders because; in that way, they become more productive and can obtain a greater amount of commodities and services for consumption. Concentrating the individual productive effort on a narrow range of goods – or even a single type of commodity or service – in the vast majority of cases pays off, since trading is often a more efficient mean of procuring goods for consumption than self-production.

According to Smith (*WN*, I.i.5, p. 17), the increase in productivity due to the division of labour can be attributed to three factors: first, 'to the increase of dexterity in every particular workman; secondly, to the saving of the time which is commonly lost in passing from one species of work to another; and lastly, to the invention of a great number of machines which facilitate and abridge labour, and enable one man to do the work of many.'

Based on his well-known proposition that the division of labour is limited by the extent of the market (*WN*, I.iii.1, p. 31)[8], Smith further argues that free trade would make a crucial contribution to the purpose of increasing the wealth of individuals and nations to the utmost, since the extension of the market beyond national borders encourages the division of labour, fosters the accumulation of capital, and spurs labour productivity at home. Thus, specialisation and free trade are intertwined with the quest for economic growth and development. In the present paper I will borrow the denomination coined by Hla Myint and refer to this benefit from trade as Smith's productivity theory.[9]

---

[7] Smith (*WN*, I.i.1, p. 13) famously states: 'The greatest improvement in the productive powers of labour, and the greater part of the skill, dexterity, and judgment with which it is any where directed, or applied, seem to have been the effects of the division of labour.'

[8] Young (1928, p. 529) considers this proposition as one of the most illuminating and fruitful generalisations which can be found anywhere in the whole literature of economics.

[9] See Myint (1958, p. 318 and 1977, p. 242).

Despite the theoretical and empirical soundness of Smith's productivity theory, for the most part of the 20th century the main framework for praising the benefits of specialisation was an alternative view commonly attributed to Ricardo. This alternative view – which Buchanan and Yoon (2002) coined as the *Ricardian logic of trade* – locates the origins of exchange in the differences among individuals or countries in terms of their capacities to produce separate final goods. According to this alternative view, trade emerges because individuals or countries have different comparative advantages in producing different goods. If such differences exist, specialisation will always prove to be mutually beneficial. If one assumes, on the contrary, that individuals or countries are identical in both their preferences and respective capacities to produce these final goods, then trade among them could not take place because it would not yield any benefits (Buchanan and Yoon 2002, p. 400).

As Buchanan and Yoon further point out, there is a subtle reversal of the logical sequence between these two alternative explanations of the origin and benefits of trade. According to the explanation provided by Smith, trade emerges because of the inherent advantages of specialisation. The observed differences among trading partners are the consequence of their respective specialisation – not the point of departure. As Smith famously wrote in the *Wealth of Nations*, the differences between a philosopher and a street porter may be small prior to their individual commitment to their respective profession (*WN* I.ii.4, pp. 28-29). In the alternative explanation currently attributed to Ricardo, though, specialisation and subsequent trade can only emerge because of inherent and pre-existing differences among potential trading partners. The interest in the exchange would continue as long as these differences persist, and would cease if the differences disappear over time.

When attributing this alternative explanation to Ricardo, it is usually assumed that the so called Ricardian trade model which can be found in contemporary economic textbooks is essentially equivalent to what is actually written in the *Principles*. As Ruffin (2002) and Maneschi (2004, 2008) have already acknowledged, though, Ricardo's demonstration of the comparative-advantage proposition is quite different from the typical textbook trade model. Thus, against what the current denomination suggests, one should not attribute the assumptions and implications of the Ricardian trade model automatically to Ricardo.

Take, for example, the constant-labour-costs assumption, upon which the whole notion about Ricardo's alternative logic of trade appears to rest. This prominent assumption of the textbook trade model stipulates that the amount of labour needed for producing a single unit of a commodity or service does not vary with the amount of commodities or services produced. The constant-labour-costs assumption is indeed incompatible with Smith's productivity theory, since the latter stipulates that an ever-increasing amount of commodities and services is produced with less amount of labour, because the division of labour and the invention and deployment of sophisticated machinery spurs labour productivity. It implies increasing returns to scale and decreasing labour costs per unit of production, not constant returns to scale.

The problem with this alleged incompatibility between the international trade theories of Smith and Ricardo is that it is based on an erroneous attribution of the constant-labour-costs assumption to the latter. The mistaken association of Ricardo with this unrealistic assumption is the consequence of the widespread – but inaccurate – interpretation of the four numbers in the famous demonstration of the comparative-advantage proposition in the *Principles* as unitary labour costs, which are assumed to remain constant. If the four numbers are interpreted accurately as the number of men working for a year required to produce some unspecified amounts of cloth and wine traded between England and Portugal, there is absolutely no need for making such an unrealistic assumption. Moreover, since the amounts of cloth and wine were not specified, it is not even possible to calculate the unitary labour costs in Ricardo's original numerical example.

So far I have not found the slightest trace of the constant-labour-costs assumption in the *Principles*. What I have actually discovered there is the complete opposite assumption, as one can appreciate in the following passage:

> 'An alteration in the permanent rate of profits, to any great amount, is the effect of causes which do not operate but in the course of years; whereas alterations in the quantity of labour necessary to produce commodities, are of daily occurrence. Every improvement in machinery, in tools, in buildings, in raising the raw material, saves labour, and enables us to produce the commodity to which the improvement is applied with more facility, and consequently its value alters. In estimating, then, the causes of the variations in the value of commodities, although it would be wrong wholly to omit the consideration of the effect produced by a rise or fall of labour, it would be equally incorrect to attach much importance to it; and consequently, in the subsequent part of this work, though I shall occasionally refer to this cause of variation, I shall consider all the great variations which take place in the relative value of commodities to be produced by the greater or less quantity of labour which may be required from time to time to produce them' (Ricardo, Vol. 1, pp. 36-37).[10]

---

[10] Throughout this paper, all direct quotations of Ricardo are extracted from *The Works and Correspondence of David Ricardo*, Volume I to XI, 2004, edited by Piero Sraffa. I will refer to them usually by indicating the volume and page numbers only.

In the above quote, Ricardo clearly affirms that the alterations in the quantity of labour necessary to produce commodities often occur on a daily basis. His assumption is, in fact, the complete opposite to constant labour costs.

4. Ricardo's Adherence to Smith's Productivity Theory

The removal of the constant-labour-costs assumption from Ricardo's demonstration of the comparative-advantage proposition is an important first step for rejecting the claim that he offered in the famous numerical example an alternative explanation of the origin and benefits of trade. As a second step, I will further argue that there is enough evidence in the *Principles* for affirming that Ricardo actually adhered to Smith's productivity theory, the core component of the explanation regarding the origin and benefits of trade in the *Wealth of Nations*. It is not too much of a stretch to imagine that Ricardo had this theory in mind when he wrote the following paragraph about the virtues of free trade in chapter 7 'On foreign trade' in the *Principles*:

> 'Under a system of perfectly free commerce, each country naturally devotes its capital and labour to such employments as are most beneficial to each. This pursuit of individual advantage is admirably connected with the universal good of the whole. *By stimulating industry, by rewarding ingenuity*, and by using most efficaciously the peculiar powers bestowed by nature, *it distributes labour most effectively and most economically:* while, *by increasing the general mass of productions,* it diffuses general benefit, and binds together by one common tie of interest and intercourse, the universal society of nations throughout the civilized world. It is this principle which determines that wine shall be made in France and Portugal, that corn shall be grown in America and Poland, and that hardware and other goods shall be manufactured in England' (Vol. 1, pp. 133–134, emphasis added).

But perhaps the best textual proof for his adherence to Smith's productivity theory is the following passage of the *Principles*, where he clearly paraphrases it:

> 'The labour of a million of men in manufactures, will always produce the same value, but will not always produce the same riches. *By the invention of machinery, by improvements in skill, by a better division of labour, or by the discovery of new markets, where more advantageous exchanges may be made, a million of men may produce double, or treble*

> the amount of riches, of *"necessaries, conveniences, and amusements,"* in one state of society, that they could produce in another, but they will not on that account add any thing to value; for every thing rises or falls in value, in proportion to the facility or difficulty of producing it, or, in other words, in proportion to the quantity of labour employed on its production' (Vol. 1, p. 273; emphasis added).

Besides making here an explicit reference to the division of labour, Ricardo also mentions two of the three factors that Smith identified as causes for an increase in productivity due the division of labour, namely the improvements in skill of the specialised worker, which Smith (*WN*, I.i.5, p. 17) calls the 'the increase of dexterity in every particular workman'; and the invention of machinery. The 'discovery of new markets' is equivalent to Smith's proposition about the extension of the market.

Ricardo explicitly deals with the effects of an extension of the market at the beginning of chapter 7 of the *Principles* when he states:

> 'No extension of foreign trade will immediately increase the amount of value in a country, although it will very powerfully contribute to increase the mass of commodities, and therefore the sum of enjoyments. As the value of all foreign goods is measured by the quantity of the produce of our land and labour, which is given in exchange for them, we should have no greater value, if by the discovery of new markets, we obtained double the quantity of foreign goods in exchange for a given quantity of our's' (Vol. 1, p. 128).

The above references to the extension of the market in the *Principles* further indicate Ricardo's agreement with Smith's productivity theory. It is well known that Smith considered the positive effects of the extension of the market on labour productivity as one of two distinct benefits of foreign trade (*WN*, IV.i.31, pp. 446-447). It is also well known that Ricardo (Vol. 1, pp. 291-295) rejected the other benefit of foreign trade mentioned by Smith, which is known in the literature as the 'vent-for-surplus' theory. If Ricardo had disagreed with both benefits, then why did he criticise and reject only one of them?

Moreover, I cannot find any evidence in the *Principles* for the suggestion that Ricardo's adherence to Smith's productivity theory is limited to the analysis of the domestic economy, because he had to recant it in his analysis of international trade due to the discovery and formalisation of the comparative-advantage proposition (Myint, 1977, p. 234). On the contrary, the repeated references to the extension of the market in chapter 7 clearly suggest that Ricardo stuck to it in his analysis of international trade.

Given the evidence of Ricardo's continuous adherence to Smith's productivity theory throughout the *Principles*, the notion that he offered an alternative and opposing logic of trade in the famous proof of comparative advantage would necessarily imply that there are two conflicting theories about the origin and benefits of trade in this book. It would mean that Ricardo was ambivalent and inconsistent in this respect, and there is no evidence for backing up such a serious charge against him.

Likewise, I do not consider Ricardo's well-known correction of Smith's views regarding the effect of foreign trade on the rate of profits in the very same chapter, as a departure or rejection of his productivity theory. Ricardo states in page 132 of the *Principles* that the rate of profits cannot be increased but by a fall in wages. For wages to permanently fall, though, the prices of the necessities on which wages are expended must fall too. Therefore, foreign trade can only have a tendency to raise the profits of stock when the commodities imported are the ones on which the wages of the labour force are expended. Thus, Ricardo does not rule out a rise in the rate of profits by the expansion of foreign trade, but rather specifies when such an increase may occur. Perhaps anticipating possible misinterpretations, Ricardo made absolutely clear in the following page that foreign trade continues to offer incentives to saving and the accumulation of capital, even in the cases when it does not increase the rate of profits:

> 'Foreign trade, then, though highly beneficial to a country, as it increases the amount and variety of the objects on which revenue may be expended, and affords, by the abundance and cheapness of commodities, incentives to saving, and to the accumulation of capital, has no tendency to raise the profits of stock, unless the commodities imported be of that description on which the wages of labour are expended' (Vol. 1, p. 133).

As he wrote a few pages earlier, 'there are two ways in which capital may be accumulated: it may be saved either in consequence of increased revenue, or of diminished consumption' (Vol. 1, p. 131).

By rejecting the notion that Smith and Ricardo had two alternative and conflicting logics of trade, I'm not denying nor belittling the fact that Ricardo disagreed with some specific propositions in the *Wealth of Nations,* related to the origin and benefits of international trade. I have already mentioned his disagreement on issues like the vent-for-surplus benefit, or the effect of foreign trade on the rate of profits. Ricardo's corrections to Smith's theory can certainly be interpreted as original and valuable contributions to the classical theory of international trade, but I do not think that they amount to an alternative and opposing theory about the origin and benefits of trade. Their mutual agreement on the productivity theory counts more heavily in this respect than their disagreement on the vent-for-surplus benefit, because the former has been traditionally considered as the primary component of Smith's theory about the origin and benefits of trade.

It might seem a bit odd that Ricardo often indicated his support for Smith's productivity theory in connection with specific critiques towards other aspects of Smith's international trade theory. A plausible explanation for this approach can be found in the general plan of the *Principles*. Ricardo conceived his book first and foremost as a compilation of propositions and insights that were either new or opposed to already established propositions of political economy. Therefore, a separate and lengthy analysis on a particular proposition or insight of Smith he agreed with, would have run against the general plan of the book.

By conceiving the *Principles* in this way, though, Ricardo may have contributed to the perception that he and Smith had divergent and incompatible explanations regarding the origin and benefits of trade. Since Smith was the highest authority in the nascent science of political economy back then, the general plan chosen artificially emphasises the differences and minimises the level of agreement with respect to Smith. Ricardo himself was well aware of this danger, as the following paragraph from the preface of the *Principles* clearly proves:

> 'The writer, in combating received opinions, has found it necessary to advert more particularly to those passages in the writings of Adam Smith from which he sees reason to differ; but he hopes it will not, on that account, be suspected that he does not, in common with all those who acknowledge the importance of the science of Political Economy, participate in the admiration which the profound work of this celebrated author so justly excites' (Vol. 1, p. 6).

Notwithstanding his awareness about the potential risk, Ricardo decided to proceed with this general plan for the *Principles* because of a personal virtue rarely seen in other famous scientists: humility. Ricardo was indeed a very humble and unpretentious man that had great self-doubts about his writing skills.[11] Because of this self-diagnosed shortcoming, he preferred to leave the major task of presenting a complete view of his ideas on political economy perhaps for a future book. Unfortunately, Ricardo died six years after the publication of the *Principles*, at the early age of 51. Contrary to his original intention, this book became the main source of his thoughts on political economy in general, and international trade in particular.

---

[11] See, for example, Ricardo's letter to James Mill (Vol. 7, p. 112) on December 20th, 1816, responding to Mill's letter of December 16th (Vol. 7, p. 106), which is equally worth reading.

From a methodological perspective, these biographical facts are highly relevant for an accurate interpretation of the main propositions in the *Principles*. These propositions cannot be accurately understood without taking into consideration the relevant passages of the *Wealth of Nations*. More importantly, one can generally presume that Ricardo agreed with those propositions of Smith which are not explicitly criticised and rejected in the *Principles*, at least until some scholar offers a convincing proof that this general presumption does not apply to a particular proposition.

5. The Relevant Cost Comparison for Specialisation and Trade

Let's turn now to the critique that Smith failed to discover the 'law' of comparative advantage as defined by the neoclassical theory of international trade. This critique is another important consequence of the widespread misunderstanding of the essence and original purpose of Ricardo's numerical example. Besides the false attribution of the constant-labour-costs assumption to Ricardo, the textbook version of the Ricardian trade model has also contributed to the spread of the popular notion that he highlighted, in the famous numerical example, a new principle or law for international specialisation known as comparative advantage. Despite investing considerable time and effort, however, I have not found in the *Principles* – or any other document written by Ricardo – the slightest evidence for such an interpretation. As has already been said, what he originally intended to illustrate with the famous four numbers was the new proposition that the labour theory of value does not regulate the relative value of commodities in international trade when the factors of production are immobile between countries. He then mentioned the associated corollary regarding comparative advantage, i.e. that a country might import a certain amount of a commodity although it can produce these commodities internally with less amount of labour than the exporting country (Morales Meoqui, 2011).

These two propositions, brilliantly demonstrated by Ricardo with a simple numerical example, are indeed significant contributions to the classical theory of international trade. First and foremost, they prove that a country may be able to export commodities to another country, even if the former incurs higher real costs of production than the importing country. This implies, of course, that a country does not need to have a productivity-advantage over the rest of the world in the production of a certain commodity in order to benefit from free trade. With the help of these two propositions one can also explain why higher real labour costs in developing countries do not command higher commodity prices in international markets. Thus, a country with relatively low labour productivity may nevertheless be the lowest nominal cost producer of a commodity. These issues are passionately contested and often misunderstood in the contemporary debate about economic globalisation.

Notwithstanding the importance and continued relevance of Ricardo's propositions, they do not constitute – nor were they ever meant to – a new principle or law for the determination of the most beneficial trade pattern between countries. Ricardo did not make use of them for this purpose in the *Principles* nor in any other document he wrote, at least as far as I know. For the determination of a country's interest in a particular exchange, he always used the classical rule of specialisation.

This rule stipulates that it is beneficial for a country to import commodities whenever it can obtain them in exchange for exports whose production entails less real cost compared to the domestic production of the same amount of the imported commodities (Viner, 1937, p. 440). The economic gains of a particular international exchange can be measured for each of the participating countries by calculating the difference between the real costs of the exported commodities that have been sent in exchange for the imports, and the expected real costs of producing the imported commodities at home. The mutually beneficial nature of international trade is secured by the prevalence of this rule in each country simultaneously. If the terms of trade or the real costs of production change in a way that the classical rule of specialisation ceases to be valid in one of the countries, this country would ultimately withdraw from this particular exchange and start producing the imported commodities at home.

In a previous paper (Morales Meoqui, 2011) I have already indicated Ricardo's recurrent use of the classical rule of specialisation in the *Principles*[12], including his famous numerical example.[13] Smith also used this rule frequently in the *Wealth of Nations*, not only for exchanges between countries, but also between individuals and regions.[14] Given the widespread use of this rule throughout the classical school of political economy, I have proposed to use this denomination instead of other popular ones like the eighteenth-century-rule or the gains-from-trade proposition.

What is the relationship between the classical rule of specialisation and the comparative-advantage proposition? Jacob Viner (1937, pp. 440-441) is essentially right when he states that the latter is an addition to, and possible implication of, the former.[15] In order to prove this implication, though, one has to assume, as Ricardo did, that the labour theory of value does not hold for international exchanges. Furthermore, Viner is also

---

[12] See, for example, Vol. 1 p. 295 and p. 319.

[13] Ricardo also used the rule in his personal correspondence, like the following letter to James Brown from October 1819 shows: 'Even with this desire for manufactures, a country might continue to be purely agricultural, if by means of trade, she could in exchange for a portion of her agricultural produce obtain a larger quantity of manufactured goods, than, with the capital employed on the production of such portion of agricultural produce as she exported, she could manufacture at home' (Vol. 8, pp. 102-103).

[14] See Smith's example of the tribe of shepherds and hunters (*WN*, I.ii.3, p. 27), the exchange between cities and the countryside (*WN*, III.i.1, p. 376), and of course foreign trade (*WN*, IV.ii.12, p. 457).

[15] Ironically, Viner's correct assessment of the relationship between the classical rule of specialisation and the comparative-advantage proposition makes more sense under the new interpretation of Ricardo's four famous numbers than under Viner's traditional interpretation as unitary costs (Viner, 1937, p. 439).

correct when he points out that the comparative-advantage proposition adds nothing to this rule as a guide for policy. This is precisely why Ricardo stated his support for free trade based on Smith's productivity theory (Vol. 1, pp. 133-134) prior to the enunciation of the comparative-advantage proposition (Vol. 1, p. 135). Therefore, it seems wrong to judge Smith's merits as an international trade theorist primarily on the basis of whether he did or did not offer a convincing proof for the comparative-advantage proposition, all the more when one might find passages of the *Wealth of Nation* where he hints at the essence of this proposition.[16]

6. Multifactorial Explanation of International Trade Patterns

Besides agreeing on the beneficial effects of the division of labour and the extension of the market on labour productivity, as well as the common use of the classical rule of specialisation, Ricardo also agreed with Smith's multifactorial approach in explaining the current pattern of international trade. This may sound surprising at first, because influential scholars behind the *New Trade Theory* – like Nobel laureate Paul Krugman (2011) – have stated that comparative advantage and increasing returns to scale are two separate and mutually exclusive explanations of the pattern of trade. This might be valid for the neoclassical theory of static comparative advantage, but not for Ricardo's notion of comparative advantage.

For any international exchange to continue over a period of time, it has to be of mutual interest for the trading partners. In order to determine whether a particular trade is indeed in the best interest of a country, one has to compare the real costs of the commodities that the country has to send abroad in order to pay for its imports, with the real costs of producing the imported commodities internally – as stipulated by the classical rule of specialisation. So when it is said that international trade patterns are determined by comparative costs, the relevant real cost comparison is invariably the one within a country – the real costs of obtaining the imported commodities from abroad

---

[16] Smith (*WN*, I.i.4, p. 16) states: 'The most opulent nations, indeed, generally excel all their neighbors in agriculture as well as in manufactures; but they are commonly more distinguished by their superiority in the latter than in the former. Their lands are in general better cultivated, and having more labour and expence bestowed upon them, produce more, in proportion to the extent and natural fertility of the ground. But this superiority of produce is seldom much more than in proportion to the superiority of labour and expence. In agriculture, the labour of the rich country is not always much more productive than that of the poor; or, at least, it is never so much more productive, as it commonly is in manufactures. The corn of the rich country, therefore, will not always, in the same degree of goodness, come cheaper to market than that of the poor.' I am indebted to Reinhard Schumacher for drawing my attention to this quote.

versus home-production – and not the real cost comparison between countries. Both Ricardo and James Mill were absolutely clear on this subject.[17]

When applying the classical rule of specialisation in a numerical example, as Ricardo did in chapter 7 of the *Principles*, it is necessary to assume that the countries involved have different relative facilities to produce the commodities traded. Otherwise, one of them would lack the gains from trade necessary for continuing the exchange under these terms, and sooner or later would abandon this unfavourable exchange. In order to illustrate the need for this assumption, I will slightly modify Ricardo's numerical example so that the amounts of cloth and wine traded between England and Portugal are produced with the same amount of labour time in the two countries:

	Number of men working for a year required to produce a given quantity of cloth and wine traded	
	cloth	wine
England	100	120
Portugal	100	120

Table 1: Numerical example without real cost differences among countries.

If the production of the amounts of cloth and wine contained in a typical trade bundle between England and Portugal requires the respective amounts of labour indicated in the above table, such an exchange might not continue for a very long time, since it is in England's but not in Portugal's interest. Portugal would gain the labour of 20 men if she starts to produce the amount of cloth at home instead of importing it from England.

Thus, the assumption about the different relative facilities of countries for producing certain commodities is indeed necessary for international specialisation, but unlike many other assumptions in economic science, this one is quite realistic. A country's ability to produce certain commodities with less real costs than another can be explained by a variety of factors, including natural conditions – such as soil, climate and geographic location – and acquired or artificial advantages, for example education, production skills, economies of scale and historical development. These factors are usually labelled in the literature as sources of comparative advantage.

In the following passage of the *Principles* Ricardo refers to the importance of achieving a better international division of labour based on the respective natural and

---

[17] Ricardo (Vol. 2, p. 383) explicitly considered the comparison of real costs between countries as irrelevant for the interest of a country in importing commodities. See also James Mill (1826, p. 123).

artificial advantages of countries: 'It is quite as important to the happiness of mankind, that our enjoyments should be increased by the better distribution of labour, by each country producing those commodities for which by its situation, its climate, and its other natural and artificial advantages, it is adapted, and by their exchanging them for the commodities of other countries, as that they should be augmented by a raise in the rate of profits' (Vol. 1, p. 132). Ricardo explicitly mentions here two natural advantages, namely climatic conditions and the geographic location of countries, but his general reference to other natural advantages suggests that he also thought of additional factors like the abundance of fertile land and raw materials.

Probably not a single economist would deny that these natural advantages are indeed important sources of real cost differences between countries, and that they certainly play a determining role in explaining the pattern of international trade. More controversial seems to be his general reference to artificial advantages. With artificial advantages Ricardo meant of course the product of human endeavour. Demand-side differences like taste and cultural traditions in specific countries, economies of scale and historical accident – all of these may be considered as artificial sources of comparative advantage.

Ricardo apparently sees no need for elaborating more specifically what he considers to be artificial advantages. Moreover, he does not even bother to differentiate between natural and artificial sources as the basis for a better international division of labour. At first glance, his approach seems to be a bit careless, because it ignores the fact that people are much more willing to accept natural rather than artificial differences. The explanation for his undifferentiated treatment of natural and artificial sources of comparative advantage has to be found in the following paragraph of the *Wealth of Nations*:

> 'Whether the advantages which one country has over another, be natural or acquired, is in this respect of no consequence. As long as the one country has those advantages, and the other wants them, it will always be more advantageous for the latter, rather to buy of the former than to make. It is an acquired advantage only, which one artificer has over his neighbour, who exercises another trade; and yet they both found it more advantageous to buy of one another, than to make what does not belong to their particular trades' (*WN*, IV.ii.15, p. 458).

Smith states in the above paragraph that the specific causes of the real cost differences – whether natural or acquired – are irrelevant for grasping the benefits from internal as well as international trade. Contemporary economists have concentrated on a narrow set of factors in order to explain why a country has greater facility in producing certain types of commodities and services than others, such as consumer tastes, a superior technology, economies of scale or the relative abundance of certain factors of production. Mainstream international trade models usually highlight a single factor and exclude all others by assumption. Such a modelling approach seems inappropriate for explaining current international trade patterns, since they are the result of several factors working simultaneously.

In the *Wealth of Nations* there are actually very interesting examples of how Smith combines natural and artificial sources of comparative advantage in order to explain the optimal pattern of trade and specialisation for the North American colonies and China. His recommendations are based on an accurate analysis of factor supplies and relative prices of the factors of production.

The North American colonies, whose Declaration of Independence in 1776 coincided with the publication of the *Wealth of Nations*, were accurately characterised by Smith as having abundant land and relative scarcity of labour and capital. In correspondence with its factor supply, rents would be generally lower and wages and profits higher in the North American colonies than in Europe. Therefore, the comparative advantage of the North American colonies would be in the production and exportation of agricultural products and raw materials rather than in the home-production of refined manufactures. Smith stated:

> 'Agriculture is the proper business of all new colonies; a business which the cheapness of land renders more advantageous than any other. They abound, therefore, in the rude produce of land, and instead of importing it from other countries, they have generally a large surplus to export. In new colonies, agriculture either draws hands from all other employments, or keeps them from going to any other employment. There are few hands to spare for the necessary, and none for the ornamental manufactures. The greater part of the manufactures of both kinds, they find it cheaper to purchase of other countries than to make for themselves' (*WN*, IV.vii.c.51, p. 609).

Imperial China, on the other hand, had abundant labour densely settled, resulting in low wages and high rents. In opposition to the economic policies of the Chinese government, which favoured agriculture more than all other employments[18], Smith identified China's comparative advantage in the production and exportation of manufactures. Furthermore, he indicated that China had probably been suffering from economic stagnation for many

---

[18] Consequently, Smith analyses the economic policies of China in the chapter about Physiocracy. See Smith (*WN*, IV.ix.40, pp. 669ff.).

centuries, having obtained the amount of wealth that its actual institutions and economic policies permit it to acquire. The expansion of foreign commerce, which China had neglected, could however give a fresh impetus to her economic development.[19]

By taking into account the relative abundance of land and labour, as well as the corresponding relative prices of these factors in the North American colonies and China, Smith clearly preceded the two Swedish economists Eli Heckscher and Bertil Ohlin, in explaining the international trade pattern based on factor endowments and relative factor prices.[20] However, instead of assuming the artificial factor endowments of a country as exogenously given, Smith was able to treat the broad pattern of changes in the factor supplies, and their relative prices, as a part of the process of long-run economic development (Myint 1977, p. 235).

It is, therefore, a well-documented fact that the two highest authorities of the classical theory of international trade, Smith and Ricardo, explicitly acknowledged plenty of sources of comparative advantage. The simultaneous operation of natural and artificial sources explains the persistent differences in real, as well as monetary, costs that give rise to the international division of labour and the observable pattern of world trade.

Moreover, it is also proven that Ricardo did not consider comparative advantage and increasing returns to scale as two separate and mutually exclusive explanations for international trade patterns. On the contrary, he considered increasing returns as an integral part of a multifactorial explanation of trade patterns based on comparative costs, whereas the relevant real cost comparison is, invariably, stated in accordance with the classical rule of specialisation.

7. Reassessment of Smith's Contributions to International Trade Theory

The main results of this paper: the evidence presented regarding Ricardo's adherence to Smith's productivity theory; the reconciliation of the comparative-advantage proposition

---

[19] See Smith (WN, I.ix.15, pp. 111-112). He also wrote: 'The home market of China is, perhaps, in extent, not much inferior to the market of all the different countries of Europe put together. A more extensive foreign trade, however, which to this great home market added the foreign market of all the rest of the world; especially if any considerable part of this trade was carried on in Chinese ships; could scarce fail to increase very much the manufactures of China, and to improve very much the productive powers of its manufacturing industry. By a more extensive navigation, the Chinese would naturally learn the art of using and constructing themselves all the different machines made use of in other countries, as well as the other improvements of art and industry which are practised in all the different parts of the world. Upon their present plan they have little opportunity of improving themselves by the example of any other nation; except that of the Japanese' (WN, IV.ix.41, p. 681).

[20] I do not mean to say by that that Adam Smith should be considered as a precursor of the neoclassical Hecksher-Ohlin trade model. The only purpose of this reference is to draw attention to the fact that although Heckscher and Ohlin are sometimes credited for incorporating natural and artificial factor endowments and relative factor prices into the explanation of international trade patterns, these issues were already present in Smith and Ricardo.

with the latter; and the reintegration of this proposition into a multifactorial explanation of the pattern of trade provided by Smith and supported by Ricardo – offer new arguments for the on-going reassessment of Smith's contributions to international trade theory. Smith has been underrated as an international trade theorist because he had failed to properly formulate and prove the comparative-advantage proposition. Ricardo's own demonstration of this proposition, though, does neither contradict nor invalidate Smith's productivity theory. On the contrary, the accurate interpretation of the numerical example in the *Principles* demonstrates quite clearly that the comparative-advantage proposition is indeed a possible implication of the classical rule of specialisation, although a very important one. Consequently, Ricardo's new proposition should be seen as a valuable addition – rather than a point of disruption – to Smith's productivity theory.

This means, of course, that Smith's valuable contributions to international trade theory cannot be belittled anymore on the basis of his shortcomings with respect to the comparative-advantage proposition. Although Smith's productivity theory remains incompatible with the neoclassical theory of static comparative advantage, there is no reason for considering the latter as the high point of free trade thinking.

Before the accurate interpretation of Ricardo's numerical example, the match-up between Smith's productivity theory and the neoclassical theory of static comparative advantage was already shifting gradually in Smith's favour. In this respect, West (1990, p. 41) argued:

> 'It is now arguable that Smith's total analysis is the more comprehensive because it goes well beyond the neoclassical reasoning. For whereas the latter simply takes as a datum an existing structure of comparative advantage, Smith's approach affords opportunities for going behind and beyond it to explain its very foundation. Manufactured instead of "natural" differences stem from incentives that prompt inherently identical individuals (or countries) to make "sunk cost" investments in an almost accidental variety of skills. In this light, many comparative advantages are man-made and the incentive for trade is an obvious development after this fact.'

Smith not only preceded Eli Heckscher and Bertil Ohlin by including natural and artificial factor endowments and relative factor prices in the explanation of the pattern of trade, but one can argue that Smith's approach was superior, since he was able to offer an endogenous explanation for the artificial factor endowments and their relative prices in particular countries, whereas the neoclassical trade theory treated them as exogenously given. Moreover, his multifactorial explanation of the pattern of trade is able to explain all sorts of trade, inter-industry as well as intra-industry.

On top of that, Smith clearly anticipated the main propositions of today's New Trade and New Growth theories. Any meticulous reader of the *Wealth of Nations* would hardly find anything completely new or particularly innovative in these two currently fashionable economic theories. The recent renaissance of Smith's insights in contemporary economic thought can be seen as a further proof for the continued relevance of his main propositions on international trade and economic growth.

After the reinsertion of Ricardo's comparative-advantage proposition into the framework of Smith's productivity theory, the match-up with the neoclassical theory of static comparative advantage seems to be overwhelmingly in favour of Smith. This might have important consequences for the mainstream theory of international trade. It may lead to a reinstatement of Smith's insights regarding the division of labour and specialisation as the foremost explanation regarding the origin and benefits of trade in contemporary economic thought.

A crucial advantage of Smith's productivity theory over the neoclassical theory of static comparative advantage is that the former offers a unified analysis of foreign trade and the domestic economy – oriented towards the problem of long-run economic growth (Myint 1977, p. 246). In classical political economy there are indeed no inherent differences in the underlying principles between domestic and foreign trade. That does not mean, however, that classical political economists ignore the existence of institutional differences between domestic and international trade, for example, different national currencies, sanitary and custom regulations or other types of administrative rules on cross-border trade. Ricardo, in particular, is certainly aware of the differences in the degrees of factor mobility within and between countries, and the resulting implications for his labour theory of value. Notwithstanding the importance of these differences between domestic and foreign trade, they do not modify the underlying logical foundation of trade.

In more practical terms, a future pre-eminence of Smith's productivity theory over the neoclassical theory of static comparative advantage would bear important implications for the contemporary political debate on free trade and economic globalisation. Smith's framework lends to a greater support for extending the division of labour and specialisation beyond political borders, since such an international extension of the market would boost labour productivity in the domestic economy. Moreover, the case for free trade based on Smith's productivity theory does not rely on unrealistic assumptions like perfect competition and constant return to scale associated with the general economic equilibrium paradigm and neoclassical theory of international trade. Critics of free trade like Graham Dunkley (2004) and Ian Fletcher (2011) have pointed to these unrealistic assumptions as a proof for the inherent weakness of the current mainstream neoclassical case for free trade. Their critique does not apply though to the classical case for free trade.

8. Conclusions

There are three important claims in this paper: first, there is enough evidence for affirming that Ricardo adhered to Smith's productivity theory; second, Ricardo's original demonstration of the comparative-advantage proposition is indeed compatible and complementary with respect to the latter; and third, that Ricardo agreed with Smith's multifactorial explanation of the pattern of trade, which includes increasing returns and economies of scale.

The notion that Smith and Ricardo had opposing and incompatible theories about the origin and benefits of international trade is largely a consequence of the widespread misinterpretation of the famous four numbers as unitary labour costs, as well as the presence of the constant-labour-costs assumption in the textbook trade model currently denominated as the Ricardian trade model. Ricardo himself, though, did not make this assumption in the original numerical example, or anywhere else in the *Principles*, for that matter. Furthermore, this notion omits the fact that Ricardo agreed with Smith's assessment regarding the importance of extending the market beyond national borders, in order to increase labour productivity and production at home, which most scholars consider as the primary benefit of foreign trade. Smith and Ricardo had significant agreements – Smith's productivity theory as well as relevant differences – the vent-for-surplus benefit, regarding the origin and benefits of trade, but their respective theories were neither alternative nor opposing.

The textbook trade model is also responsible for the erroneous notion that Ricardo proposed a new law of international specialisation called comparative advantage. The accurate understanding of the numerical example in the *Principles* proves, beyond doubt, that he relied upon the same rule of specialisation as Smith and other classical political economists for defining the interest of a country in a particular exchange, as well as measuring the gains from trade.

Since a complete assessment of the overall compatibility of the numerous contributions made by Smith and Ricardo to the theory of international trade cannot be accomplished with the necessary rigour in the limited space available in a typical research paper, the present paper merely focused on proving the three claims mentioned above. Nevertheless, the results of this partial assessment suggest that the level of compatibility between the theories of international trade of Smith and Ricardo is significantly higher than it is currently reflected in the economic literature.

Finally, the proof of Ricardo's adherence to Smith's productivity may perhaps contribute to the reestablishment of the latter as the main explanation of the benefits of free international trade. Those who believe in the virtues of free trade should embrace such a development, since the reliance of the mainstream neoclassical case for free trade on unrealistic assumptions like constant returns to scale or perfect competition has given the numerous critics of free trade an easy target to rally against.

Acknowledgements

I'm thankful for the valuable comments provided by Farhad Rassekh on an earlier version of this paper. I would also like to thank Reinhard Schumacher and Alexandre Laino Freitas for their worthy reviews and valuable suggestions in the Open Peer Discussion forum. The remaining errors and inconsistencies though are all mine.

References

Aldrich, J. (2004) The Discovery of Comparative Advantage. *Journal of the History of Economic Thought*, 26(3), pp.379–399.

Blecker, R.A. (1997) The "Unnatural and Retrograde Order": Adam Smith's Theories of Trade and Development Reconsidered. *Economica*, 64(255), pp.527–537.

Bloomfield, Arthur I. ([1975] 1994) Adam Smith and the Theory of International Trade. In Arthur Bloomfield, ed. *Essays in the History of International Trade Theory*. Cheltenham, UK and Northampton, USA: Edward Elgar, pp. 109-144.

Bloomfield, Arthur I. (1989) Aspects of the Theory of International Trade in France: 1800 – 1914. *Oxford Economic Papers*, 41(3), pp. 619-639.

Buchanan, J.M. & Yoon, Y.J. (2002) Globalization as Framed by the Two Logics of Trade. *The Independent Review*, 6(3), pp.399–405.

Dunkley, G. (2004) *Free Trade*, London: Zed Books.

Elmslie, B. (1994a) Positive feedback mechanisms in Adam Smith's theories of international trade. *The European Journal of the History of Economic Thought*, 1(2), pp.253–271.

Elmslie, B. (1994b) The endogenous nature of technological progress and transfer in Adam Smith's thought. *History of Political Economy*, 26(4), pp.649–663.

Elmslie, B. & James, A.M. (1993) The Renaissance of Adam Smith in Modern Theories of International Trade. In R. F. Hébert, ed. *Perspectives on the History of Economic Thought*. Aldershot: Edward Elgar, pp. 63–76.

Fletcher, I. (2011) *Free Trade Doesn't Work* 2nd ed, Sheffield, MA: U.S. Business & Industry Council.

Kibritçioğlu, A. (2002) On the Smithian origins of "new" trade and growth theories. *Economics Bulletin*, 2(1), pp.1–15.

Krugman, P.R. (2011) Increasing Returns in a Comparative Advantage World. In R. M. Stern, ed. *Comparative Advantage, Growth, and the Gains from Trade and Globalization: A Festschrift in Honor of Alan V. Deardorff.* Singapure: World Scientific Publishing Co. Pte. Ltd., pp. 43–51.

Krugman, P.R. (1990) *Rethinking International Trade*, Cambridge, Mass.: The MIT Press.

Krugman, P.R. (2009) The Increasing Returns Revolution in Trade and Geography. *The American Economic Review*, 99(3), pp.561–571.

Krugman, P.R. (1993) The narrow and broad arguments for free trade. *The American Economic Review*, pp.362–366.

Kurz, H.D. (1992) Adam Smith on Foregin Trade: A Note on the"Vent-for-Surplus" Argument. *Economica*, pp.475–481.

Kurz, H.D. (1997) What Could the "New" Growth Theory Teach Smith or Ricardo? *Economic Issues*, 2(2), pp.1–20.

Maneschi, A. (2008) How Would David Ricardo Have Taught the Principle of Comparative Advantage? *Southern Economic Journal*, 74(4), pp.1167–1176.

Maneschi, A. (2004) The true meaning of David Ricardo's four magic numbers. *Journal of International Economics*, 62(2), pp.433–443.

Mill, J. (1826) *Elements of Political Economy* Third, London: Baldwin, Cradock, and Joy.

Morales Meoqui, J. (2011) Comparative Advantage and the Labor Theory of Value. *History of Political Economy*, 43(4), pp.743–763.

Myint, H., (1977) Adam Smith's Theory of International Trade in the Perspective of Economic Development. *Economica*, 44(175), pp.231–248.

Myint, H. (1958) The "classical theory" of international trade and the underdeveloped countries. *The Economic Journal*, 68(270), pp.317–337.

Rassekh, F. (2012) The Theory of Comparative Advantange in Smith's *Wealth of Nations*. Manuscript. University of Hartford.

Ricardo, D. (2004) *The Works and Correspondence of David Ricardo.* Vol. I-XI. Edited by P. Sraffa, Indianapolis: Liberty Fund Inc.

Roberts, R. (2010) Roberts on Smith, Ricardo, and Trade [online]. Available from: http://www.econtalk.org/archives/2010/02/roberts_on_smit.html [Podcast]. [Accessed 25 April 2013].

Ruffin, R.J. (2002) David Ricardo's discovery of comparative advantage. *History of Political Economy*, 34(4), pp.727–748.

Ruffin, R.J. (2005. Debunking a myth: Torrens on comparative advantage. *History of Political Economy*, 37(4), pp.711–722.

Smith, A. (1976) *An Inquiry into the Nature and Causes of the Wealth of Nations* R. H. Campbell & A. Skinner, eds., Indianapolis: Liberty Classics.

Sraffa, P. (1930) An alleged correction of Ricardo. *The Quarterly Journal of Economics*, 44(3), pp.539–544.

Viner, J. (1937) *Studies in the Theory of International Trade*, London: Allen & Unwin.

West, E.G. (1990) *Adam Smith and Modern Economics*, Edward Elgar Pub.

West, E.G. (1978) Scotland's resurgent economist: a survey of the new literature on Adam Smith. *Southern Economic Journal*, 45(2), pp.343–369.

Young, A.A. (1928) Increasing returns and economic progress. *The Economic Journal*, 38(152), pp.527–542.

SUGGESTED CITATION:

Morales Meoqui, J. (2014) 'Reconciling Ricardo's Comparative Advantage with Smith's Productivity Theory'. *Economic Thought*, 3.2, pp. 21-37.
http://www.worldeconomicsassociation.org/files/journals/economicthought/WEA-ET-3-2-MoralesMeoqui.pdf

The Theory of the Transnational Corporation at 50+

Grazia Ietto-Gillies[1], London South Bank University and Birkbeck University of London, UK
iettogg@lsbu.ac.uk

Abstract

The paper briefly summarises the historical evolution of transnational corporations (TNCs) and their activities. It then introduces the major theories developed to explain the TNC. There is an attempt to place the theories historically, within the context of the socio-economic conditions and of the relevant economic ideas in which they were developed. The following theories are discussed: Hymer's, market power and control; Vernon's international product life cycle; the internalisation theory; Dunning's eclectic framework based on Ownership, Location, and Internalisation (OLI) advantages; The Scandinavian School; the evolutionary approaches of Cantwell and of Kogut and Zander; the New Trade theory applied to the TNC; the role of nation-states in the strategic behaviour of TNCs. There are some critical comments at the end of each presentation. A brief analysis of key elements in the theories, their differences and commonalities follows. It is pointed out that the pattern of development shows tensions between the following interconnected elements: (1) contents and methods of interest to Business Schools and to Economics Departments; (2) static versus dynamic approaches; (3) emphasis on efficiency versus strategic elements; (4) strategies towards rivals as well as towards other players in the economic system such as labour, governments and suppliers; (5) single- *versus* multi-disciplinary approaches; and micro *versus* macro approaches.

Keywords: transnational corporations, Hymer; Vernon, internalisation theory, Dunning, Scandinavian School, Cantwell, Kogut and Zander, New Trade theory and multinationals, nation-states and transnationals, history of economic ideas

1. Introduction

The theory of the transnational corporation (TNC) [2] and of its defining activity – foreign direct investment (FDI) – were born with the seminal doctoral dissertation of Stephen

---

[1] A version of this paper was presented at the 17th Annual Conference of the European Society for the History of Economic Thought (ESHET) on *Economic Theory and Business Practice: Their Relations Through the Ages*, Kingston University, London 16-18 May 2013.

[2] A variety of adjectives and nouns are used to indicate this particular type of firm. Adjectives include 'international', and 'multinational'; the nouns include: 'firm', 'company', 'corporation', 'enterprise'. I prefer the

Hymer (1960 [1976]). Prior to it there have been theories of cross-border movements of capital and theories of imperialism[3]. The TNCs as such played no part in either. Theories about international capital movements were developed within the neoclassical tradition and following, mainly, the framework of neoclassical theories of trade, specifically Heckscher (1919) and Ohlin (1933)[4]. The theories of imperialism were developed within the Marxist tradition, whether the relevant authors maintained their Marxists roots or not (Hobson, 1902; Luxemburg, 1913; Lenin, 1917; Bukharin, 1917).

What has been developed since Hymer's work is a variety of theories dealing with different aspects of the TNC. Their focus ranges from: why firms become transnational; to the modalities of their activities; to FDI as their main activity; to why some countries become host or home (or both) for TNCs and FDI.

This paper considers the main theories, developed since Hymer's, which have the TNC as a focus. The next section gives a brief excursion into the activities of the TNCs in the twentieth century and beyond. Section three summarises the main theories by presenting them – as far as possible – in historical sequence. Section four analyses the key elements in the theories presented in section three. Section five summarises and concludes.

2. TNCs and Their Activities in History[5]

The antecedents of the modern TNC can be traced very far back into history. Transborder direct business activities go back many centuries, indeed before the formation of nation-states. The Medici Bank can be considered a company with such direct business activities. In later centuries, the chartered companies such as the East India Company, The Royal African Company and the Hudson Bay Company had some elements in common with the present TNCs but the differences are too large for them to be seen as forerunners. Hymer (1971), following Chandler (1962), traces back the origin of the TNC in joint stock companies established from the mid-nineteenth century. But what is the distinguishing characteristic of modern TNCs compared to previous companies?

The distinguishing way of doing business abroad, the one that characterises the transnationals compared with other companies, is *direct* production and generally direct business activities abroad. In order to engage in these direct activities, the TNCs establish affiliates abroad and acquire the ownership and control of their assets. This

---

adjective 'transnational' because it conveys the fact that these corporations can organise, manage and control activities across countries rather than just operate in several of them independently.
[3] A summary of those pre-WWII theories is in Ietto-Gillies (2012, Part II).
[4] Other main contributions are Nurkse (1933) and Iversen (1935).
[5] For a more extensive treatment of the issue discussed in this section see Ietto-Gillies (2012, Part I).

gives them a long-term interest in the strategies and management of the foreign enterprises which they control. But what do we mean by control?

Control is usually seen as ownership control: what percentage of ownership secures a majority in decision making[6]. While percentage ownership remains the main element in the exercise of control we should point out two qualifications. First, as Cantwell notes in his Comments – it is possible for the contemporary large TNC to exercise control over a network of externalised activities performed in independent firms over which the TNC has no ownership control. This is a point raised by Cowling and Sugden (1987; 1998) as well as Dunning and Lundan (2008). Second, ownership control, in itself, may not be sufficient to exercise full control by management. For the latter to be able to fully control the activities of their company two requirements are necessary: (a) a good system of communications and transportation; and (b) appropriate internal organisation of the company. Innovations of the technological and organisational types have made it possible to secure such control and therefore they have made it possible for the modern TNCs to develop and grow from the 20th century onward.

The growth in the number of TNCs worldwide and in their operations has progressed steadily after the Second World War. The increase has been very considerable since the mid-1970s. In 1968–9 the number of TNCs originating from 14 developed countries was 7276 (Ietto-Gillies (2002a, p. 12, table 2.1). This figure is likely to be very close to the total number of world TNCs at the time. The latest World Investment Report (UNCTAD, 2012; statistics table 34) estimates the total number of TNCs worldwide to be 103,786.

Various elements have contributed to the growth of TNCs and their activities, specifically the following: (a) The developments in transportation and in communications technologies and costs. (b) The organisational innovation within large companies and institutions. (c) The favourable political environment after the Second World War. (d) The liberalisation and privatisation programmes of many developed and developing countries in the last 30 years.

Elements (a) and (b) have made control at a distance possible. Moreover, they have led to lower costs including the cost of inventory holding[7]. All four elements together have greatly facilitated and encouraged companies to invest abroad. There has been large growth in the value of FDI worldwide as well as in the growth of other modalities of internationalisation for which TNCs are responsible: from trade to licensing, to franchising to joint ventures. The growth in the number of transnationals and in their activities is also reflected in changes in the sectoral structure and connected changes in the geographical structure of TNCs' activities. Between WWI and WWII most FDI was by resource-seeking

---

[6] This is indeed the basis on which the IMF (1977) distinguishes between foreign direct investment (FDI) – 10+ percent holding – and portfolio investment – less than 10 percent.

[7] See Cantwell (2014) and also Iammarino and McCann (2013, ch.3.3, pp. 90-95).

TNCs and therefore most FDI was in developing countries. After WWII most FDI was in manufacturing. It was by developed countries' TNCs and directed towards other developed countries: for example, a manufacturing US corporation investing in the UK or Canada.

The development of information and communications technologies (ICTs) has allowed the vertical division of the production process and the location of various components into different type of countries; labour intensive components located in developing countries and those requiring the high skills and latest technologies located in developed countries. From the late 1970s onwards we have seen a surge of FDI in services directed to both developed and developing countries. In terms of modalities the first few decades after WWII saw most of FDI taking the greenfield – i.e. real investment and accumulation – mode. From the 1980s onwards most FDI has taken the mergers and acquisition (M&A) modality (UNCTAD, 2000). The different pattern has implication for competition as well as for the level of activity and employment in the host country.

Regarding the political environment (elements c and d above), the post WWII decades have seen considerable changes. The 1960s and 1970s were seen as decades of *confrontation* between TNCs and national governments, particularly those in developing countries. There were large numbers of nationalisations of foreign affiliates, particularly in developing countries. As neoliberalism took hold and spread we saw confrontation slowly turning into *cooperation* between national governments and TNCs (Dunning, 1993, ch. 13). Far from threatening nationalisations, many governments in developing and east European countries followed in the footsteps of some developed countries in engaging in large-scale privatisations. The privatised assets were often bought by foreign companies. UNCTAD (1993, fig. 1, p. 17) shows that the number of nationalisations peaked in the mid-1970s and became non-existent after the mid-1980s. Privatisations started in the mid-1970s and increased very rapidly in the 1980s and 1990s. The 1990s saw a wave of protests by anti-globalisation movements against international institutions at the heart of globalisation and neoliberalism including TNCs. The protests faded away leaving few traces[8]. Neoliberalism led to the big financial crisis of 2007-08. The austerity policies that followed have recently (2012-13) led to questions about the tax arrangements of TNCs via their transfer prices policies.[9]

The next section will discuss the main theories put forward to explain these developments.

---

[8] The new wave of protests (in Turkey and Brazil) in the last few years are indirectly focused on TNCs and globalization issues.
[9] On transfer prices and their effects see Ietto-Gillies (2012, ch. 20) as well as Eden (2001).

3. The Main Theories[10]

Hymer's Seminal Work

Stephen Hymer was a Canadian economist doing doctoral research at the Massachusetts Institute of Technology in Cambridge, USA. He became intrigued by the motivations behind the large foreign investment by US corporations in a growing number of countries including his own. He died in a car accident in 1974, aged 39, and his dissertation was published posthumously in 1976. Hymer's work constitutes a radical departure from the conventional neoclassical approach of the time. It opened a whole new research programme in the area of international production. Follow-ups, refinements and new twists to the theory are continuously coming out.

In order to understand the relevance of Hymer's contribution, as well as the novelty of his approach, we must remember that, when he was writing, there was no theory of foreign direct investment as such. There was no perceived need to consider direct investment as a special case; indeed the concept of foreign direct investment had not been developed before Hymer's breakthrough. The then prevalent neoclassical theory explained movements of capital across borders via differentials in interest rates. However, as Hymer noted:

- FDI does not necessarily involve movement of funds from the home to the host country. In fact, direct investment is, at times, funded in other ways including borrowing in the host country or via retained profits.
- FDI often takes place both ways so that both countries involved are originators and hosts to FDI.
- FDI tends to be concentrated in particular industries across various countries, rather than in a particular country across various industries.

These three characteristics are incompatible with the neoclassical explanation for movements of capital based on differentials in interest rates. Hymer thus saw the need to differentiate between purely financial investment (i.e. from portfolio investment) and investment by large firms for production purposes. His demarcation criterion between foreign direct investment and portfolio investment is *control*. Direct investment gives the firm control over the business activities abroad; portfolio investment does not. By acquiring control of foreign assets the firms removes conflicts with local competitors. It does so by giving the controlling firm more market power and thus intensifying the

---

[10] The theories presented in this section as well as other theories are discussed at greater length in Ietto-Gillies (2012, Part III). See also Cantwell (2000).

imperfections in the market structure. The existence of structural market imperfections is, in fact, one of the key assumptions of Hymer's theory: market imperfections and the search for market power are a key determinant of FDI. Moreover, market power is affected by companies' strategies including the ones leading to control of foreign assets and production. The types of imperfections he considers are structural ones, that is, those imperfections arising from the market structure, for example from an oligopolistic structure in which a few large firms dominate the market.[11]

Later works by Hymer are more in the Marxist tradition. They emphasise the contradictory and conflictual nature of capitalist production and deal with the following issues.

  (a) Effects of MNCs' activities on: labour; politics; the nation-state and its government.
  (b) The effectiveness of economic policies (Hymer, 1966; 1975; Cohen et al., 1979, chs 9 and 11).
  (c) The division of labour (Hymer, 1970, 1971; 1972; Cohen et al., 1979, ch. 6) within the firm, the industry and the international arena (in particular between developed and developing countries).

Vernon's International Product Life Cycle

Raymond Vernon was working on what became a well-known theory at the same time as Hymer and indeed up the road from where Hymer was working: at the Harvard Business School. The economic context of Vernon's theory is one of expanding technologies and markets for new mass consumption products such as washing machines. It was also one of increased internationalisation as barriers to movements of products and capital gradually came down after WWII. The theoretical background to his approach must be sought in the technological gap theories of trade (Posner, 1961) and in the theories of the product's life cycle (Kutznets, 1953). In fact, while Hymer's point of departure is the firm, Vernon's is the product. How new products emerge; how they impact on the innovating firm and to the industry structure in which the firm operates; how the firm is affected by the progress of the product through its life; how the product progresses through its life in national and international markets and production locations.

Vernon begins with the assumption that enterprises in any one of the advanced countries of the world have equal access to knowledge. However, this does not mean an equal probability of application of such knowledge to the development of new products. It is the consciousness of opportunities and the responsiveness to such opportunities that vary from one entrepreneur to another. Such consciousness and responsiveness are

---

[11] Transactional imperfections – à la Coase - are considered by Hymer (1968), a paper which seems to have little relationship with his main work (1960 [1976]) and with his later research.

associated with the market conditions in which entrepreneurs operate; this makes knowledge inseparable from the decision-making process about its use. Therefore knowledge is not an exogenous variable.

In the 1960s and 1970s the US market offered unique opportunities for the exploitation of knowledge and its embodiment in new products because:

- It was a market in which consumers had high average income per capita.
- It was a very large market; hence even minority tastes were likely to provide a fairly large market.
- It was characterised by high unit labour costs and a large supply of capital; it was, in other words, a market abundant in capital and scarce in labour.

For these reasons the new product would be located in the US. Such location would secure flexibility of adaptation to possible problems and to requirements of consumers. Adaptation is more easily achieved if production takes place near its initial development location. Moreover, when first launched into the market, the product enjoys a large amount of differentiation and thus a semi-monopolistic position. It will have low price elasticity of demand and high income elasticity.

However, as the product matures and the market expands there will be the threat of imitators. Expanding foreign demand – usually in other developed countries – will first be met by exports. At a later stage direct production in Europe may replace exports in response to the following: the emergence of competitors in European countries; possible import controls; and possible lower production costs in Europe. As the product becomes standardised, competition increases and the search for lower production costs starts. This last phase in the life of the product is likely to lead to the location of production in developing countries and to the sourcing of developed countries' markets – including the US itself – from this production.

The key elements in Vernon's highly dynamic theory are: innovation in products which gives the firm a temporary monopolistic position; interaction between the life of the product, the degree of competition in the industry and the geography of trade and of FDI/production.

Many criticisms can be levelled at the theory[12]. It was developed in the 1960 and reflected the economic environment of the times as Vernon himself recognised in a courageous article which dissects critically his own theory (1976). Moreover, as time went by, not only the economic environment and the differences between the US and European economies changed, we also saw significant technological changes. The development and wider effects of ICTs brought shorter product lives as well as changes

---

[12] See, for example, Cantwell (1995).

in the sequences of location of international production. Moreover, it should be noted that the concentration of the theory on the product more than on the firm does not allow a full analysis of the competitive position of the firm and how it can be affected by product diversification strategies.

The Internalisation Theory

The post war expansion in Western economies saw concentration of production and increase in firms' size. Concomitantly with – as a consequence of – these developments companies adapted their organisational systems to cope with new functions, new products or new geographies in the more complex resultant structures.

The internalisation theory of the TNC reflects these changes in the economic environment. It was developed on the back of Coase's analysis of the firm (1937) and it also benefitted from Williamson's later developments (1975; 1981). It started with a paper by McManus (1972); a fuller development was achieved with Buckley and Casson (1976). Further contributions include Teece (1977); Rugman (1981); Caves (1982) and Hennart (1982).

Buckley and Casson concentrate on a particular type of market imperfection: transaction imperfections as in Coase's analysis. When markets present transactional imperfections there is an incentive to internalise. Why do firms internalise? What are the limits to internalisation? There are benefits of internalisation and there are also costs; the balance between the two will determine the limit to internalisation[13]. The benefits of internalisation stem from *transactional market imperfections* and relate to one or more of the following situations.

- When there are long time lags between initiation and completion of the production process and, at the same time, futures markets are non-existent or unsatisfactory.
- When the efficient exploitation of market power over an intermediate product requires discriminatory pricing of a kind difficult or impossible to implement in an external market, though possible to implement internally.
- When imperfections would lead to bilateral concentration of market power and thus to an unstable situation under external markets.
- When there is inequality in the position of the buyer and seller regarding knowledge on the value, nature and quality of the product; the resultant buyer uncertainty may encourage forward integration.

---

[13] This equilibrium approach to the firm is taken up by the New Trade theories applied to the TNC as discussed below.

- When there are imperfections deriving from government intervention in international markets – such as the existence of *ad valorem* tariffs, restrictions on capital movements, discrepancies in rates of taxation.

The two most important areas of internalisation relevant to TNCs are *markets for intermediate products* and *markets for knowledge*. Before the Second World War the major factor that contributed to the emergence of multinational enterprises (MNEs) was demand for primary products, leading to vertical integration across frontiers and to internalisation of intermediate markets. Since WWII the major factor has been the growth in demand for knowledge-based products coupled with the difficulties of organising efficient external markets for intangibles and knowledge. A TNC implies internalisation across national boundaries. Buckley and Casson (1976, p. 45) write on this issue: 'There is a special reason for believing that internalization of the knowledge market will generate a high degree of multinationality among firms. Because knowledge is a public good which is easily transmitted across national boundaries, its exploitation is logically an international operation.' So the conclusions seem to be that imperfect markets generate incentives to internalise; the market for knowledge is highly imperfect, so there are strong benefits in internalising it.

The internalisation theory of the TNC is still a very successful and widely used theory. However, there are some doubts about it. There is the question of whether the theory is tautological as the authors themselves recognise. Casson (1982, p. 24) writes: 'Internalization is in fact a general theory of why firms exist, and without additional assumptions it is almost tautological.' Buckley (1983, p. 42) expresses similar doubts when he writes: 'At its most general, the concept of internalisation is tautological; firms internalise imperfect markets until the cost of further internalism outweighs the benefits.'

In terms of relationship with the economic context to which the theory is supposed to apply the following should be noted. When the theory was first developed, there had been decades of firms' growth via internal expansion leading to concentration and large firms in many industries. However, the last 30 years have seen a great increase in outsourcing and generally in firms' activities being contracted out and bought on the market. Yet, these are the decades when the internalisation theory has been most successful within the international business community. The two macro patterns – decades of internalisation followed by decades of externalisation – cannot be explained by the same theory of internalisation[14] though the theory can explain the choice between internalisation and externalisation at the level of firms.

Moreover, the following should be noted. The internalisation theory tries to explain why – and in what circumstances – firms prefer the FDI rather than licensing route

---

[14] See Cantwell (2014) and Ietto-Gillies (2014) for a further discussion on this issue.

to growth, thus why they prefer internalisation to market-based relationships. However, even accepting that internalisation is to be favoured because it cuts transactional costs, it is not clear why firms should prefer the FDI rather than the exporting route: the first implies internalisation across borders; the latter modality implies internalisation within the nation-state.

Dunning's OLI Advantages

John Dunning worked on international production issues from the 1950s onwards and until his death in 2009. His early research was on the factors leading to the high productivity of American investments in British manufacturing. In his (1977) he developed a 'systemic' theory – whose origin he traces to his earlier work (Dunning, 2000b) – designed to explain internationalisation modes and processes. He developed a framework for considering: (a) all main modalities of internationalisation and specifically FDI, exports and licensing thus attempting to address the criticism of the internalisation theory mentioned in the last paragraph of the previous subsection; (b) issues of why and when firms invest in foreign countries; and (c) issues of why certain countries become attractive for inward FDI.

Dunning's wide framework was built around the analysis of three sets of advantages: Ownership, Locational and Internalisation (OLI) advantages.

1. *Ownership advantages* are those that are *specific to a particular enterprise*.[15] They constitute competitive advantages towards rivals and enable the company to take advantage of investment opportunities wherever they arise. This set of advantages links Dunning's theory to Hymer's.

2. *Locational advantages* are those advantages *specific to a country* which are likely to make it attractive for foreign investors.

3. *Internalisation advantages* are all those benefits that derive from producing internally to the firm; they allow it to bypass external markets and the transaction costs associated with them. They are, essentially, benefits of operating within *hierarchies rather than markets*. This set of advantages links Dunning's theory to the internalisation theory and, of course, to Coase's theory of the firm.

Foreign direct investment takes place whenever:

- The enterprise concerned possesses '…net ownership advantages *vis-à-vis* firms of other nationalities in serving particular markets' (1980, p. 275).

---

[15] I agree with John Cantwell (2014) when he points out that ownership advantages is a wider concept than firm-specific advantages. The former includes those advantages that the firm derives from the macro and national environment.

- The enterprise derives benefits from internalising the use of resources in which it has an advantage rather than selling them on external markets, e.g. via licensing.
- The country where the FDI takes place must offer special locational advantages to be used in conjunction with those deriving from *ownership* and *internalisation*.

Dunning's theory has been for many years – and still is – the main reference framework for many pieces of international business research. It gives a clear, well defined framework which gives scope for micro-meso-macro analyses and for multi- and inter-disciplinary approaches. Its multi-variable structure makes it easy to apply to almost any country, firm and time. Each of the above three sets of advantages (OLI) can include a long list of variables from which researchers can choose in the adaptation of their research to the specific context they are interested in. Thus the theory seemed to be always applicable independently of specific circumstances. This wide applicability made the theory irrefutable and rather than strengthen it, may have weakened it. A theory that is always applicable may be tautological and loses its usefulness and scientificity. Moreover, most of the criticisms that were levelled at the internalisation theory apply also to Dunning's because it also relies on internalisation. Nonetheless, Dunning's wide framework has the enduring virtue of adaptability and flexibility (Cantwell, 2014). Moreover, it lends itself to multi-level and interdisciplinary analyses.

Dunning was well aware of the weaknesses of his framework and, in later years, further developed it. He also worked on many other aspects of international business. Specifically he developed important work in the following areas:

- Operationalisation via contextualisation of the three sets of variables (Dunning, 1993a and 2000a).
- Dynamisation (Dunning, 1993b) of his eclectic theory.
- The relationship between international production and countries' development patterns (Dunning, 1981, ch 5; Dunning and Narula, 1996).
- Incorporations into the framework of new and growing organisational forms such as mergers and acquisitions and inter-firm collaborative agreements (Dunning, 1997).

The Scandinavian School

The international business researchers we have discussed so far concentrated on countries which have been traditionally involved in FDI such as the US and UK. However, the 1960s and 1970s also saw many other countries involved in international direct production. A group of Swedish economists and management/marketing/strategy academics (Johanson and Wiedersheim-Paul, 1975; Johanson and Vahlne, 1977 and

1990) became interested in studying the position of smaller countries and their companies' strategies towards international activities. Their interest focuses on strategies in relation to the stages and modalities of internationalisation that companies go through. The authors link the stages and modalities to the timing of internationalisation activities. The timing determines the modality of establishment of operations abroad; it also affects the amount invested and the type of country in which the operations are established, starting with the nearest countries in terms of both spatial and psychic distance.

The authors analyse two internationalisation patterns. The first one is designed to explain the increasing involvement in a single foreign country. The second pattern explains involvement in a variety of countries. The theory is very dynamic in that it considers time sequences and also because the resources already committed in a country impact on further decisions. Thus, decisions about the future modalities, countries and the amount of resources to be committed abroad depend on the path already followed in internationalisation in terms of resources committed, modalities followed and countries of involvement.

The conclusion is that involvement in any single foreign country will proceed cautiously and in accordance with the following stages in the establishment chain:

- exports via agents;
- setting up of sales subsidiaries;
- setting up of production subsidiaries.

The above sequence is the result of state and change aspects in which knowledge and uncertainty play a large role. The dynamic sequence is linear in two ways: because each stage leads to the next one and because each new stage involves a larger commitment of resources than the previous stage.

The *second internationalisation pattern* refers to the spread of internationalisation *from one foreign country to others*. Here the sequence is also dynamic and linear proceeding by stages from the foreign country(ies) psychically closer to those more distant. Psychic and spatial distances tend to be strongly related.

The dynamism in the theory links it to Vernon's. Both theories consider stages and time sequences. In Vernon's case the stages relate to the life of the product and they affect its production location and its markets. They also impact on the competitive environment in which the firm operates at the various stages in the product life. In the case of the Scandinavian School the stages refer to the modalities and locations of internationalisation. This is a theory not about the product, but about the firm and its internationalisation strategies. The relationship between the product – in terms of innovativeness, technology or potential demand – and the firm is not considered; neither is the market structure in which the firm operates.

Evolutionary Approaches to the Theory of the TNC

Coase (1937) questioned the firm-market relationship and the reasons for the very existence of the firm. However, questions about the internal functioning of the firm and its objectives were left unanswered or, indeed, were not asked at all: the firm continued to be a black box. Its opening started with Penrose (1956) – a work that had very little impact when first published though it is now, deservedly, recognised – and with Nelson and Winter (1982), a work that had a considerable impact since publication.

Neither of these two works dealt directly with the multinational company. However the competence-based theory of the firm which they expounded had a big impact on other authors working on international business and specifically on John Cantwell as well as on Kogut and Zander.

Cantwell (1989) takes on the competitive advantages view of Hymer and of Dunning but goes a step further. He considers such advantages not as exogenous but as created by the firm itself. Specifically they can be created in the field of innovation and technology within which the firm becomes the generator of its own advantages. The theory is thus injected with: (a) realism, because it attempts to answer the question: where do advantages come from? and (b) dynamism because it links created advantages to changes within the firm and its environment.

According to Cantwell, the TNCs are in a particularly strong position to develop their ownership advantages in innovation. By operating in many countries – often characterised by diverse knowledge and innovation contexts – they can acquire knowledge from the localities and use it to further their innovative activities. In this process the TNC is aided by its involvement in two types of networks: (1) its own internal network between the various units of the firm spread in a variety of geographies; and (2) external networks between units of the firm and suppliers/distributors, consumers and partners in collaborative ventures[16].

The latter networks enable units of the TNC to acquire knowledge from their external environment. This knowledge is incorporated within the unit and also transferred to other units of the TNC via its internal network. The TNC, with its geographically diversified structure, its variety of organisational interactions with the external environments and its internal network, is in the best position to accumulate innovation and technology across countries and through time. The internal networks raise issues of control of the subsidiaries by the headquarters of the company. The external networks raise issues of the degree of embeddedness of the subsidiary into the local economy. The acquired knowledge gives the TNC advantages in all its modalities of operation from

---

[16] The links between internal and external networks and knowledge diffusion have been explored in the management/organisational analysis literature (Forsgren at al., 2005; Hedlund, 1986; Hedlund and Rolander, 1990; Bartlett and Ghoshal ,1988 and 1991; Ghoshal and Nohria, 1997).

FDI to export to licensing. Here is one of the several criticisms of the internalisation theory on the part of Cantwell: in the real world, FDI and exports are complementary not an 'either/or' situation. There is an empirical basis to this criticism since the TNCs are responsible not only for all FDI but also for over three quarters of world trade (UNCTAD 2013, fig. IV.14 and Box IV.3, pp. 135-6). Moreover, over one third of world trade is intra-firm, i.e. between different units of the same company though across different countries.

Thus knowledge spills over from the locality to the TNCs. It also spills over from the TNC to the local economy. The absorptive capacity of the locality becomes crucial for the innovation benefits for both the local economy and the unit of the TNC operating within it. There is a dynamic interaction and a cumulative causation mechanism between ownership advantages and locational advantages and both can be seen as endogenous and created. Thus the separation of ownership from location advantages in Dunning's OLI framework may be misleading.

Kogut and Zander's analysis focuses on the role played by knowledge in the boundaries of the firm, i.e. the extent to which the firm decides to expand via internalisation or through external, contractual relationships. Kogut and Zander start by criticising the standard view on the boundaries of the firm: the internalisation theory. In the latter the boundaries are set by the failure of the market to protect knowledge and by market transaction costs. Moreover, in the internalisation view the boundaries of the firm are independent of its ownership advantages.

Kogut and Zander's (1993) key insights are the views of (a) the firm as a social community and (b) the development of knowledge as a product of the social group. They write: '...firms are social communities that serve the efficient mechanisms for the creation and transformation of knowledge into economically rewarded products and services'. In Kogut and Zander (2003, p. 511) we read on this point: '...knowledge exists in networks and in institutionalized contexts.'

Whenever knowledge is embedded in – and dependent on – social structures, it is more context-specific and, largely, tacit. This makes it less likely to be codifiable, teachable and transferable to other social settings. The social community setting of knowledge development means that: (a) knowledge is more likely to be tacit because emerging from shared experiences and procedures; and (b) further knowledge development is likely to emerge from the shared experiences. Here we have clear pointers towards the fact that the social nature of the firm and of groups within it lead to a specific type of knowledge and to ownership advantages and value creation. The authors write: 'Cooperation within an organization leads to a set of capabilities that are easier to transfer within the firm than across organizations and constitute the ownership advantages of the firm.' (p. 627). The social community setting of the firm applies also to the TNC because its subsidiaries tend to share identities and values or, at least, they share them to a higher degree than each subsidiary would share with independent external firms.

For Kogut and Zander, the limits to the firm are, therefore, set not by market failure but by the firm's efficiency in acquiring knowledge. They write: 'In our view, firms are efficient means by which knowledge is created and transferred [...]. Through repeated interactions, individuals and groups in a firm develop a common understanding by which to transfer knowledge from ideas into production and markets. In this very critical sense, what determines what a firm does is not the failure of the market, but the firm's efficiency in this process of transformation relative to other firms' (p. 631).

Moreover, the authors see knowledge as the main source of ownership advantages and there is, therefore, interaction between ownership advantages and internalisation. The ownership advantage characteristic of knowledge is enhanced by the fact that tacit, uncodifiable knowledge is also more difficult to imitate: knowledge is therefore an advantage on which the firm can further build up without fears from rivals' imitations.

Knowledge is cumulative. Older knowledge is more easily codifiable and therefore more easily transferable outside the boundaries of the firm. The costs of technology transfer vary with the degree of tacitness of the related knowledge. Thus established technology is not a public good; it is transferable at a cost and the cost varies with the accumulation of experience and learning about codification procedures.

As knowledge becomes more codifiable with the passage of time, the company is likely to move from internalisation to externalisation, from FDI to licensing in international operations. The sequence and its timing depend on the degree of tacitness and codifiability of the knowledge specific to the firm.

These two evolutionary theories have much in common as well as many differences. Cantwell's approach is very critical of the internalisation theory while Kogut and Zander's is, ultimately, a theory of why firms internalise. Their view is that the limits to internalisation and thus the boundaries of the firm are not set by transactional market failures – as in Coase and in the internalisation theory – but by the efficiency of the firm in developing, spreading and utilising knowledge. Both theories can be seen to have elements of created ownership advantages and thus of market power. However, the impact on – and interaction with – the local economy so prominent in Cantwell is absent in Kogut and Zander.

New Trade Theories and the TNC

The evolutionary theory of the firm was an attempt to move the theory of the TNCs more towards the real world and away from the neoclassical theory of the firm. It was also an attempt to inject into the theory elements from disciplines other than economics and more in line with organisational sociology (Kogut and Zander). Meanwhile other forces were pushing more towards the directions of an 'economics-only' theory of the TNCs and one more strongly embedded into partial equilibrium analysis and the neo-classical framework. The 1980s saw the development of New Trade theories (Krugman, 1985; 1991a; 1998) in which the trade pattern could be linked to increasing economies of scale and its advantages for countries on the basis of their factor endowments[17]. These developments gave way to a considerable amount of research in which the New Trade theories and their models could be used to explain regional development and agglomeration as well as developed versus developing countries' trade. They were also used to draw policy implications from those analyses.

This framework, however, cannot explain direct production in other countries by TNCs. Essentially, if there are external economies of agglomeration and the internal economies are plant economies, then it can only make sense to produce in one location/country and supply other markets through exports. There is a basic conflict and tension between a theory that predicts clustering of production activities and a reality of companies that spread their activities in space – sometimes horizontally, sometimes vertically, sometimes both ways.

At the theoretical level it is possible to solve the conundrum by adjusting some of the assumptions, and this is what some economists have done. The assumption of capital immobility – underlying much trade theory – has obviously to be removed when dealing with theories of direct foreign production and FDI, which by their nature imply capital mobility. Moreover, constraints on the movements of products are sometimes introduced, such as barriers to trade.

However, the main adjustment is in the treatment of *internal economies of scale*. They are split into two types:

- internal economies at the level of plants
- internal economies at the level of the firm.

These economies separately or together are of the Chamberlinian type i.e. they are internal to the firm. They are therefore analysed in the context of imperfect competition. The first type of economies – those at the plant level – are linked to more traditional fixed inputs, those deriving from traditional physical assets such as machinery; they give rise to fixed costs. The second type of economies derives from such inputs and assets as organisational, technological, managerial/marketing; the services deriving from them are of benefit to – and can be used by – the company as a whole, and therefore by its head

---

[17] The modelling of equilibrium under economies of scale became possible after the development of the mathematics behind imperfect competition and increasing returns (Dixit and Stiglitz,1977).

office as well as by its affiliates. These are *joint inputs within the firm* because they can be used by different parts of the firm for the same product and/or for different products. No matter how many plants (and affiliates) are going to use these inputs, the marginal cost of using the inputs in additional plants – at home or abroad – is low or negligible. In addition to this, the industry as a whole may also achieve scale economies of the external, Marshallian type.

The authors dealing with this specific theory in the context of TNCs have developed models for FDI from developed countries directed towards (a) other developed countries (Markusen, 1984 and 1995); and (b) developing countries (Helpman, 1984 and 1985; Helpman and Krugman, 1985). This is done by changing the assumptions.

These highly theoretical models do not seem to fit the facts very well. Krugman (1998, p. 15) writes: 'preliminary efforts . . . have found that such models are not at all easy to calibrate to actual data; in general, the tendency toward agglomeration is stronger in the models than in the real economy!'

There are several problems and contradictions within the overall framework. They go from using a Chamberlinian monopolistic competition framework for companies that operate under oligopolistic condition; to the lack of consideration for exports as an alternative to FDI. This is a point in common with the internalisation theory which is the starting framework for the New Trade theories. It is a problematic point because – as we saw above – TNC are responsible for most world trade as well as for all FDI.

In my view the most problematic element is the fact that the analysis is largely a spatial analysis: transport costs play a big role in the outcome of where different plants will be located. It is essentially a theory of spatial location of production – a field that geographers have been interested in for decades. As such it does not distinguish between plant location within a single nation-state or across nation-states. In other words, the nation-state is hardly relevant in the New Trade theories.

The Role of Nation-States

I have argued elsewhere (Ietto-Gillies, 2012, ch.14) that the existence of nation-states is the very reason why we need theories of the TNC as opposed to theories of the firm in general. Yet the nation-state – as determinant of TNCs' activities if not in terms of effects on it – has, largely, been ignored by most theories. Hymer did write on the State and the nation-state and their interaction with the international firm. This was part of his post-dissertation research which had a Marxist orientation. He was particularly interested in the effects of TNCs' activities on the abilities of national governments to develop and implement policies. However, Hymer did not consider the relevance of the nation-state for the explanation of TNCs and FDI.

Nation-states are relevant because they are characterised by different regulatory regimes[18] regarding (a) labour and social security systems; (b) fiscal systems; (c) currencies; (d) industrial policies including incentives to businesses; and (d) environmental and safety standards. The differences in these regulation regimes allow companies that can truly organise, manage and control their operations transnationally to arrange their activities so as to benefit from these differences. Their transnationality puts them in a position of advantage towards actors – with whom they interact – who are not able to operate transnationally, or not to the same extent. Such actors include: labour; governments of nation and regional states; suppliers. Moreover, their international operations allow them, also, to build up advantages in terms of risk spreading and of acquisition of knowledge from the various localities in which they operate.

Transnationality therefore gives the TNC the ability to develop strategies that maximise their bargaining power towards other actors such as labour, governments or suppliers. In particular, labour working for the same company in countries with differing labour law, trade unions and social security systems cannot organise effectively – or not as effectively – as if it were all working for the very same company within the same country. These strategies of transnationality thus result in a strategy of fragmentation of labour by national geographies. Moreover, in the last 30 years there have also been strategies of organisational labour fragmentation. Outsourcing strategies lead to labour working for a variety of companies and have thus weakened its bargaining power. Outsourcing can take the international route via offshoring strategies. The organisational fragmentation of labour can, in this case, combine with geographical (by nation-state) fragmentation.

It was pointed out above how the internalisation theory cannot explain the trend towards externalisation in the last three decades. This trend can only be explained if we bring in socio-political-economic elements linked to reactions to the power of labour vis-à-vis large corporations. Outsourcing and externalisation in general were developed from the 1980s onwards as organisational strategies leading to the fragmentation of labour and thus to its lower bargaining power. Such power had increased in earlier decades characterised by internalisation.

Thus, a full study and understanding of TNCs require them to be placed in the context of nation-states. Moreover, it requires their analysis to be made in terms of strategic rather than efficiency/equilibrium behaviour. Strategic behaviour has, at times, been considered in the literature on firms and TNCs. But it is usually in the context of strategies towards rival firms. Hymer's, Dunning's and Cantwell's analyses of firms' advantages can be seen in the context of advantages and strategic behaviour towards

[18] Here we focus on regulatory regimes only. There are, however, other differences between nation-states as discussed in Ietto-Gillies (2012). See Cantwell (2014) and Ietto-Gillies (2014), both in this issue, for further discussions on cultural and regional differences.

rival companies. These are certainly very important. However, it is also worth stressing advantages with respect to other players in the economic system from labour to governments to suppliers. Advantages with respect to any of those will result in higher profits and thus also in advantages with respect to rivals.

4. Key Elements in the Theories and their Context

As with theories in any other field, the ones we discussed above must be seen in the economic and social context in which they were developed. They must also be seen in the context of the ideas and theories prevalent at the time. These elements have been pointed out in the subsections above. Nonetheless there are also elements specific to the TNC theories and to some of these elements we now turn.

The theories here presented are only a subset of all those developed to explain the TNC and its activities. However, they are the ones which have been most successful in terms of acceptance by the research and pedagogy community[19]. Such a community does not coincide with the economics academic community. In fact, theories of the TNC have been most successful within the wider international business community. This is a very large and active community mostly clustered around Business Schools or a variety of Business Departments from Marketing and Strategy to Organisational Analysis to Economic Geography. Economics Departments have – largely – ignored the theory of the TNC following the very first rejection of Hymer's work. Why should that have been so? Why the neglect of an institution that has been so relevant to economies and societies particularly after WWII? I can only attempt to guess possible reasons: perhaps the feeling that there is nothing special about the TNC over and above the large corporation; or the difficulty of analysing messy institutions characterised by various locations and types of activities and slotting them into neat categories and analyses particularly of the mathematical type. It is interesting, therefore, to note that the strictly economics community has taken an interest in the TNC and developed the New Trade theory applied to TNCs when they were able to develop neat, equilibrium models of it. These are not very realistic but they can be taught as part of the general economic curriculum[20].

Against economics-only theories there have been theories developed with reference to other disciplines from marketing – Vernon as well as the Scandinavian School – to sociology of organisations – Kogut and Zander and, to some extent, Cantwell. One effect of the multidisciplinary contexts is the fact that the methodologies used tend to

---

[19] This statement does not apply to the theory presented in the last sub-section.

[20] A very clear textbook (Barba Navaretti and Venables, 2004) has been developed explaining TNCs and their activities entirely in terms of the New Trade theory applied to the MNCs. No mention is made of the historical development of TNCs nor of other explanations for their emergence, development and activities.

be more wide ranging and diversified compared to that which one normally sees in the economics-only type of theories. They range from traditional econometrics to qualitative methods based on large scale or on selected, in-depth interviews.

Moreover, the emphasis of theories developed in multidisciplinary contexts tends to be wider than the purely efficiency/equilibrium analysis of economics. Strategic elements are brought in, usually with reference to company's strategies towards rivals. However, strategies towards other players in the economic system – labour, governments and suppliers – can also be brought in to reflect their relevance for the pattern of internationalisation.

Whether developed in the context of Economics or Business studies, the theories can differ in terms of their dynamic versus static approaches. Those developed by Vernon, the Scandinavian School and Cantwell have definitely more dynamic elements; in the case of Vernon and Cantwell the dynamic elements are endogenous to their theories.

Most theories emphasise – directly or indirectly – market imperfections and market power. However, these can be of two types: structural imperfections in which large TNCs operate in imperfect markets and have varying degrees of market power sometimes endogenously built by their own strategies (as in Cantwell's theory). Imperfect markets can be – directly or indirectly – traced down to oligopolistic structures (Hymer; Dunning; Cantwell) or to monopolistic competition (Vernon; New Trade theories). Imperfections may also be of the transactional type, à la Coase. The internalisation theory – Buckley and Casson; Dunning – falls into the latter category.

It should also be noted that the theories vary in terms of what it is that they are trying to explain: from FDI only; to a variety of modalities of international business; to the TNC as a firm; to patterns of FDI; to the position of different countries vis-à-vis FDI and transnational companies. Earlier theories and writers – Hymer, Vernon, Dunning – straddled between micro, meso and macro analyses (Cantwell, 2014); an approach consistent with the fact that one is dealing mostly with very large companies. However, other writers and theories moved the focus almost exclusively towards the micro level (the internalisation and the Scandinavian theories as well as Kogut and Zander). This writer's view is that the micro and macro are never as interrelated as when we study the behaviour and strategies of TNCs. It follows that we must consider them together – as in the last subsection of Section 3 – if we want to understand what is going on in contemporary economies.

5. Summary and Conclusions

The paper briefly summarises the historical evolution of TNCs and their activities. It then introduces the major theories developed to explain the TNC. The presentation is in historical sequence. There is also an attempt to place each theory in its socio-economic and history of ideas contexts. The following theories are discussed. Hymer, market power and control; Vernon's international product life cycle; the internalisation theory; Dunning's eclectic framework based on: Ownership, Location, and Internalisation (OLI) advantages; the Scandinavian School; the evolutionary approaches of Cantwell and of Kogut and Zander; the New Trade theory applied to the TNC, the role of nation-states in the strategic behaviour of TNCs. There are some critical comments at the end of each presentation. A brief analysis of key elements in the theories, their differences and commonalities follows in Section four. It is pointed out that the pattern of development shows tensions between the following interconnected elements: (1) contents and methods of interest to Business Schools and to Economics Departments; (2) static versus dynamic approaches; (3) emphasis on efficiency versus strategic elements; (4) strategies towards rivals as well as towards other players in the economic system such as labour, governments and suppliers; (5) and single- versus multi- and interdisciplinary approaches; (6) micro versus meso versus macro level analyses.

The transnational companies dominate our economies and more research should be devoted to them by the economics community. I firmly believe that such a community would benefit from multi- and interdisciplinary links with relevant fields as well as from a historical and history of ideas approach to the field. I also believe that equilibrium analyses may be inappropriate to such institutions and that reality should be at the forefront of analysis. It may also be time for economists working in paradigmatic approaches, other than the neo-classical one, to take a more active interest in this key actor of contemporary economies.

Acknowledgements

The welcome Commentary by John Cantwell in this issue has led to some modifications of the original paper. I would like to thank the editors of this journal for very helpful suggestions.

References

Barba Navaretti G. and Venables, A. J. (2004) *Multinational Firms in the World Economy*, Princeton and Oxford: Princeton University Press,

Bartlett, C.A., Ghoshal, S. (1991) *The Transnational Solution*. Cambridge, MA: Harvard Business School Press.

Buckley, P. J. and Casson, M. C. (1976) A long-run theory of the multinational enterprise. In Buckley, P. J. and Casson, M. C. (eds), *The Future of the Multinational Enterprise*, London: Macmillan, 32-65.

Cantwell, J. (1989) *Technological Innovation and Multinational Corporations*. Oxford: Blackwell.

Cantwell, J. (1995) 'The globalisation of technology: what remains of the product cycle model?', *Cambridge Journal of Economics*, 19 (1), 155–74.

Cantwell, J. (2000) 'A survey of theories of international production', in C.N. Pitelis and R. Sugden (eds), *The Nature of the Transnational Firm*, London: Routledge, pp. 10–56.

Cantwell, J. (2014) 'A commentary on Grazia Ietto-Gillies' paper, *"The Theory of the Transnational Corporation at 50+"*, *Economic Thought 3.2, pp 58-66.*

Caves, R.E. (1982) *Multinational Enterprise and Economic Analysis*, Cambridge: Cambridge University Press.

Chandler, A.D. (1962) *Strategy and Structure: Chapters in the History of the Industrial Enterprise*, Cambridge, MA: MIT Press.

Coase, R.H. (1937) 'The nature of the firm', *Economica*, 4 386–405; reprinted in G.J. Stigler and K.E. Boulding (eds) (1953), *Readings in Price Theory*, London: Allen and Unwin, pp. 331–51.

Cohen, R.B., Felton, N., van Liere, J. and Nkosi, M. (eds) (1979), *The Multinational Corporations: A Radical Approach. Papers by Stephen Herbert Hymer*, Cambridge: Cambridge University Press.

Cowling, K. and Sugden, R. (1987) *Transnational Monopoly Capitalism*, Brighton: Wheatsheaf.

Cowling, K. and Sugden, R. (1998) 'The essence of the modern corporation: markets, strategic decision-making and the theory of the firm', *The Manchester School*, 66 (1), 59–86.

Dixit, A. and Stiglitz, J. (1977), 'Monopolistic competition and optimum product diversity', *The American Economic Review*, 67, 297–308.

Dunning, J. H. (1977) Trade, location of economic activity and the MNE: a search for an eclectic approach. In Ohlin, B., Hesselborn, P. O. and Wijkman, P. M. (eds), *The International Allocation of Economic Activity*, London: Macmillan, 395-431.

Dunning, J.H. (1980) 'Explaining changing patterns of international production: in defence of the eclectic theory', *Oxford Bulletin of Economics and Statistics*, 41 (4), 269–95.

Dunning, J.H. (1981) *International Production and the Multinational Enterprise*, London: Allen and Unwin.

Dunning, J.H. (1993a) *Multinational Enterprises and the Global Economy*, Wokingham: Addison Wesley.

Dunning, J.H. (1993b) *The Globalization of Business*, London: Routledge.

Dunning, J.H. (1997) *Alliance Capitalism and Global Business*, London: Routledge.

Dunning, J.H. (2000a) 'The eclectic paradigm as an envelope for economic and business theories of MNE activity', *International Business Review*, 9, 163–90.

Dunning, J.H. (2000b) 'The eclectic paradigm of international production: a personal perspective', in C. Pitelis and R. Sugden (eds), *The Nature of the Transnational Firm*, London: Routledge, pp. 119–39.

Dunning, J.H. and Lundan, S.M. (2008) *Multinational enterprises and the Global Economy*, second edition, Cheltenham, UK and Northampton, MA, USA: Edward Elgar.

Dunning, J.H. and Narula, R. (1996) 'The investment development path revisited: some emerging issues', in J.H. Dunning and R. Narula (eds), *Foreign Direct Investment and Governments, Catalysts for Economic Restructuring*, London: Routledge.

Eden, L. (2001) Taxes, Transfer Pricing, and the Multinational Enterprise, in A.M. Rugman and T.L. Brewer (eds), *The Oxford Handbook of International Business*, Oxford: Oxford University Press, ch. 21, pp. 591-619.

Forsgren, M., Holm, U. and Johanson, J. (2005) *Managing the Embedded Multinational. A Business Network View*, Cheltenham, UK and Northampton, US: Edward Elgar.

Ghoshal, S. and Bartlett, C.A. (1988) 'Innovation processes in multinational corporations', in M.L. Tushman and W.L. Moore (eds), *Readings in the Management of Innovation*, Cambridge, MA: Ballinger, pp. 499–518.

Ghoshal, S. and Nohria, N. (1997) *The differentiated MNC: Organizing Multinational Corporations for Value Creation*, San Francisco, CA: Jossey-Bass.

Heckscher, E. (1919) 'The effect of foreign trade on the distribution of income', in H. Ellis and L.A. Metzler (eds) (1950), *Readings in the Theory of International Trade*, London: Allen and Unwin, pp. 272–300.

Hedlund, G., (1986) The hypermodern MNC – a heterarchy? *Human Resource Management*, 25(1): 9-35.

Hedlund, G. and Rolander, D. (1990) 'Action in heterarchies: new approaches to managing the MNC', in C.A. Bartlett, Y. Doz and G. Hedlund (eds), *Managing the Global Firm*, London: Routledge, pp. 1–15.

Helpman, E. (1984) 'A simple theory of international trade with multinational corporations', *Journal of Political Economy*, 92 (3), 451–71.

Helpman, E. (1985) 'Multinational corporations and trade structure', Review of Economic Studies, July, 443–58.

Helpman, E. and Krugman, P. (1985) *Market Structures and Foreign Trade: Increasing Returns, Imperfect Competition and the International Economy*, Cambridge, MA: MIT Press.

Hennart, J.-F. (1982) *A Theory of Multinational Enterprise*, Ann Arbor, MI: University of Michigan Press.

Hymer, S. H. (1960, published 1976) *The International Operations of National Firms: a Study of Direct Foreign Investment*, Cambridge, MA: MIT Press.

Hymer, S.H. (1966), 'Direct foreign investment and the national economic interest', in P. Russell (ed.), *Nationalism in Canada*, Toronto: McGraw-Hill, pp. 191–202.

Hymer, S.H. (1968) 'La grande "corporation" multinationale: analyse de certaines raisons qui poussent à l'integration internationale des affaires', *Revue Economique*, 14 (6), 949–73; English version ('The large multinational "corporation": an analysis of some motives for the international integration of business') in M. Casson (ed.) (1990), *Multinational Corporations*, Aldershot, UK and Brookfield, USA: Edward Elgar, pp. 6–31.

Hymer, S.H. (1970) 'The efficiency (contradictions) of multinational corporations', *American Economic Review*, 60 (2), 411–18; reprinted in R.B. Cohen, N. Felton, J. Van Liere and M. Nkosi (eds) (1979), *The Multinational Corporation: A Radical Approach, Papers by S.H. Hymer*, Cambridge: Cambridge University Press, pp. 41–53.

Hymer, S.H. (1971) 'The multinational corporation and the law of uneven development', in J.W. Bhagwati (ed.), *Economics and World Order*, London: Macmillan, pp. 113–40; reproduced in H. Radice (ed.) (1975), *International Firms and Modern Imperialism*, Harmondsworth: Penguin, pp. 113–35.

Hymer, S.H. (1972) 'The internationalisation of capital', *The Journal of Economic Issues*, 6 (1), 91–111.

Hymer, S.H. (1975) 'The multinational corporation and the law of uneven development', in H. Radice (ed.), *International Firms and Modern Imperialism*, Harmondsworth: Penguin Books, pp. 113–35.

Iammarino, S. and McCann, P. (2013) *Multinationals and Economic Geography. Location, Technology and Innovation,* Cheltenham, UK and Northampton, MA, USA: Edward Elgar.

Ietto-Gillies, G. (2012) *Transnational Corporations and International Production. Trends, Theories, Effects*, 2nd edition, Cheltenham, UK and Northampton, MA, USA: Edward Elgar.

Ietto-Gillies, G. (2014) *'Reply to John Cantwell's Commentary on Grazia Ietto-Gillies' paper: "The Theory of the Transnational Corporation at 50+"*, Economic Thought 3.2, pp. 67-69.

International Monetary Fund (IMF) (1977) *Balance of Payments Manual*, 4th edition, Washington, DC: IMF.

Iversen, C. (1935) *International Capital Movements*, 1967 edition, London: Frank Cass.

Johanson, J. and Vahlne, J.-E. (1977) 'The internationalization process of the firm – a model of knowledge development and increasing foreign market commitment', *Journal of International Business Studies*, 8 (1), 23–32.

Johanson, J. and Vahlne, J.-E. (1990) 'The mechanism of internationalization', *International Marketing Review*, 7 (4), 11–24.

Johanson, J. and Wiedersheim-Paul, F. (1975) 'The internationalization of the firm: four Swedish cases' *Journal of Management Studies*, October, 305–22.

Kogut, B. and Zander, U., (1993) 'Knowledge of the Firm and the Evolutionary Theory of the multinational Corporation' *Journal of International Business Studies*, 4th quarter: 625-45.

Krugman, P. (1985) 'Increasing Returns and the Theory of International Trade', *National Bureau of Economic Research Working Papers*, No. 1752, November.

Krugman, P. (1991a) *Geography and Trade*, Cambridge, MA: MIT Press.

Krugman, P. (1998) 'What's new about the new economic geography?', *Oxford Review of Economic Policy*, 14 (2), 7–17.

Kutznets, S. (1953) *Economic Change*, New York: W.W. Norton.

Markusen, J.R. (1984) Multinationals, multiplant economies and the gains from trade. *Journal of International Economics* 16 (3/4), 205-24. Reprinted Bhagwati, J.N. (ed.) (1981). *International Trade: Selected Readings*. Cambridge, MA: MIT Press, 457-95.

Markusen, J.R. (1995) 'The boundaries of multinational enterprises, and the theory of international trade', *Journal of Economic Perspectives*, 9 (2), 169–89.

McManus, J. (1972) 'The theory of the international firm', in Gilles Paquet (ed.), *The Multinational Firm and the Nation State*, Don Mills, Ontario: Collier-Macmillan, pp. 66–93.

Nelson, R.R. and Winter, S.G. (1982) *An Evolutionary Theory of Economic Change*, Cambridge, MA: Harvard University Press.

Nurkse, R. (1933) 'Causes and effects of capital movements', in J.H. Dunning (ed.) (1972), *International Investment*, Harmondsworth: Penguin, pp. 97–116.

Ohlin, B. (1933) *Interregional and International Trade*, 1967 edition, Cambridge, MA: Harvard University Press.

Penrose, E. T. (1956) 'Foreign Investment and the Growth of the Firm' *The Economic Journal*, 66, 262: 220-35.

Rugman, A.M. (1981) *Inside the Multinationals: The Economics of the Multinational Enterprise*, New York: Columbia University Press.

Teece, D.J. (1977) 'Technology transfer by multinational firms: the resource cost of transferring technological know-how', *The Economic Journal*, 87, 242–61.

United Nations Conference on Trade and Development (UNCTAD) (1993), *World Investment Report 1993. FDI Policies for Development: National and International Perspectives*, Geneva: United Nations.

United Nations Conference on Trade and Development (UNCTAD) (1996) *World Investment Report 1996: Investment, Trade and International Policy Arrangements*, Geneva: United Nations.

United Nations Conference on Trade and Development (UNCTAD) (2000) *World Investment Report 2000.Cross-border Mergers and Acquisitions and Development*, Geneva: United Nations.

United Nations Conference on Trade and Development (UNCTAD) (2012) *World Investment Report 2012. Towards a New Generation of Investment Policies*, Geneva: United Nations.

United Nations Conference on Trade and Development (UNCTAD) (2013) *World Investment Report 2013. Global value Chains: Investment and Trade for Development*, Geneva: United Nations.

Venables, A.J. (1998) 'The Assessment: Trade and Location' *Oxford Review of Economic Policy*, 14, 2: 1-6.

Vernon, R. (1966) 'International investment and international trade in the product cycle', *The Quarterly Journal of Economics*, 80, 190–207.

Vernon, R. (1979) 'The product cycle hypothesis in a new international environment', *Oxford Bulletin of Economics and Statistics*, 41, 255–67.

Williamson, O. (1975) *Markets and Hierarchies: Analysis and Anti-trust Implications*, New York: Free Press.

Williamson, O.E. (1981) 'The modern corporation: origins, evolution, attributes', *Journal of Economic Literature*, 19, 1537–68.

SUGGESTED CITATION:

Ietto-Gillies, G. (2014) 'The Theory of the Transnational Corporation at 50+'. *Economic Thought*, 3.2, pp. 38-57.
http://www.worldeconomicsassociation.org/files/journals/economicthought/WEA-ET-3-2-Ietto-Gillies.pdf

A commentary on Grazia Ietto-Gillies' paper: 'The Theory of the Transnational Corporation at 50+'

John Cantwell, Rutgers University, Newark, New Jersey, USA
cantwell@business.rutgers.edu

Keywords: transnational corporations, Hymer, Vernon, internalisation theory, Scandinavian School, Cantwell, Kogut and Zander, New Trade theory and multinationals, nation-states and transnationals, history of economic Ideas

---

This paper offers a splendid overview and a succinct summary of the theory of international business. It should be especially helpful for Ph.D. students in this field, and perhaps for other scholars that are coming into the area from other specialisms, or considering doing so. The article extends the author's recently revamped book, *Transnational Corporations and International Production: Trends, Theories, Effects* (Ietto-Gillies, 2012), which book I commend and indeed which I use myself as a central text on my own doctoral course in the Theory of International Business. The author knows already of my views on many of the issues she discusses, both because she refers to some of my earlier work in the paper, and from some direct correspondence that we had in the past over her book, when she was writing it or re-writing it.

Ietto-Gillies is right to recognise that the issues addressed by the theory have altered over the 50+ years as the environment has changed, and with it the nature of the subject; and by the migration of the subject from departments of economics, and to a slightly lesser degree from departments of marketing and of finance, to becoming incorporated in its own right in business schools – most often within departments of management and sometimes in standalone departments of international business. I detect in the paper some sense of disappointment on the part of the author that the subject areas of economics and international business have diverged over the period described. As Ietto-Gillies has described, the theory of international business was spawned from economics a little over 50 years ago. The subsequent narrowing of the discipline of economics that has moved it away from the domain of international business studies will be well known to World Economics Association members. The philosophically deep, historically rich and complex thinking of scholars such as John Dunning or Dick Nelson, impoverished if overly formalised, which was so welcomed in the economics profession of the 1960s (or in any earlier era) would not be so welcome today. Nelson has termed what has been lost or relegated to a secondary place within the economics discipline as 'appreciative theory' (see e.g. Nelson, 1998). Appreciative theory is closer to the complexity of real-world social and economic systems – and to their changing historical context – than is the deductive logic, axioms and more restrictive assumptions of formal theory. Evolutionary economics in the tradition of Nelson and Winter, in common with international business studies, has instead returned to the traditions of classical political economy in relying on appreciative theory as the primary driver of analysis that explains real-world processes, and which, in modern terminology, we would call multidisciplinary and interdisciplinary in nature.

International business as a subject area has moved steadily further down this road of multidisciplinary theory-building grounded on empirical observation, despite adopting some quantitative methods that simplify relationships and which come with a language taken from certain natural science contexts (hypothesis testing and controls) that is questionable when applied to complex social systems in which we cannot conduct controlled experiments. However, since formal representations of international business theory tend to be associated with quantitative applications, they are also designed to have a direct connection with some aspect of empirically observed phenomena (rather than model-building for its own sake, not directly linked to any observation, as in much neoclassical economic theory). The purpose of this formal structure of tests against the evidence is generally seen as a capacity to draw conclusions that have conceptual implications which feed into the enrichment of, and the new contribution to, some relevant appreciative theory. As Nelson argues, when a subject is progressing well, there is a largely positive and constructive relationship between appreciative theory and formal theory, or formal representations of relationships. Given this relative openness of the international business subject area, it is not surprising that inputs have been accommodated or absorbed from beyond economics, and especially from those working on the sociology and psychology of management.

Ietto-Gillies and I can agree that it would indeed be wonderful if the broader approach of classical political economy, driven by appreciative social and behavioural science theorising, were to be revived beyond the realm of international business studies, and to be embraced – as it once was – in economics as a whole. However, in at least some specialised fields of study, such as in international business, in innovation studies, in much evolutionary economics, and in some economic history, this traditional form of approach has been preserved and revitalised. It would be welcome for it to return to the economics discipline as a whole at some stage, but the discussion of this aspiration lies beyond the scope of our present exchange.

Ietto-Gillies does a good job of showing how the theory of international business has evolved in terms of the analysis of its dominant actor, the transnational corporation (TNC), and in evaluating the strengths and weaknesses of the various components of that theory that have emerged along the way. I would add the interpretative comment that the

theory has become steadily more multi-level as it has moved from macro level appraisals to incorporate more micro elements. This of course is related to the points I have made already, about the move from economics and finance towards management and strategy, and interest in more micro and individual aspects of the subject from scholars with backgrounds in sociology or psychology. While Hymer and Dunning began by analysing patterns of foreign direct investment (FDI) at the country and industry level, and Vernon explained cross-country patterns of trade and FDI, those such as Buckley and Casson or Johanson and Vahlne shifted attention to the firm level, and the more recent scholarship of those like Birkinshaw has brought this down to the firm sub-unit or subsidiary level. More recently still, work has begun at the project level, which is appropriate where intra-firm networks become increasingly interconnected with inter-organisational networks, as hinted at in Ietto-Gillies's reference to the trend away from internalisation and towards externalisation (outsourcing, subcontracting and the like). Our theories of international business need increasingly to be adapted to handle a synthesis of these various levels. While it is quite common to discuss multi-level analysis simply in terms of the required statistical methodology, the point I would emphasise here is that it calls for theory which is complex and multi-disciplinary in nature. Therefore, it is unsurprising that the trends in the international business field towards the explicit incorporation of different levels of analysis on the one hand, and towards more multidisciplinary and interdisciplinary approaches on the other, have gone hand in hand with one another.

The recognition of a change in the international business environment from internalisation towards externalisation leads me to two other comments on Ietto-Gillies's article. First, Ietto-Gillies is right to draw attention to the conflation of ownership and control in the literature on international business from Hymer onwards. As conveniently also reflected in the definition of FDI used by the agencies responsible, an ownership stake in a business abroad above some threshold share of equity is supposed to be both necessary and sufficient to ensure control over the management of that (thus) subsidiary company. In the earlier era of internalisation it seemed quite appropriate to associate the ownership of assets with the capacity to control the use of those assets. Of course, it was always understood that sometimes such control might not be actively exercised despite the existence of a majority holding, or equally sometimes control might be exercised over enterprises such as dependent suppliers despite a lack of ownership in their business, but these were often regarded as minor qualifications – the exceptions that merely proved the rule. Today, however, we must acknowledge that firms often exercise control over much wider international business networks in forms that are commonly known as 'global production networks' or 'global value chains', in which substantial parts of the network or chain are not owned, but are effectively controlled or orchestrated by the flagship firm. This led Dunning, for example, in his later work, to shift away from the traditional definition of the TNC in terms of the ownership of income-generating assets abroad, and towards defining the TNC instead as a firm that takes the lead responsibility for the orchestration of international business networks (see e.g. Dunning and Lundan, 2008).

I mention this not because of any novelty about Dunning's definition of the firm or TNC in terms of its network of control rather than its ownership of assets – this idea and discussions around it have been around for a long time – but rather because the Dunning and Lundan account shows how this conceptualisation of the TNC has now become central to mainstream thinking in the international business field. However, while many of us found conceptually attractive the Cowling and Sugden (1987) definition of the TNC in terms of the strategic coordination of production facilities across national borders, it has to be admitted that it is very difficult to operationalise this definition empirically, and this problem remains unresolved. This is why in most empirical work the firm continues to be treated as a legal entity that owns assets and employs people, which is usually how it is also required to report its operations as a firm, and it is not generally defined as the coordinator of a network of business activity that ranges well beyond the facilities it owns and the people it directly employs, through a variety of formal (contractual) and informal (cooperative) relationships. It may well be that, to empirically operationalise the construct of an informal business network coordinated by a TNC, we need to work at the project level rather than at the firm or corporate level, especially since these networks depend often on decentralised structures of coordination (unlike in the earlier Cowling and Sugden definition of the firm in terms of coordination from a single centre).

As an aside, the new trade theories discussed by Ietto-Gillies are less able to explain the spread of global production networks than are the new firm-level approaches to international trade that have emerged from more empirically oriented economists working on trade and TNCs (e.g. Feinberg and Keane, 2006). In this perspective, which is echoed in recent work in international economic geography (see Iammarino and McCann, 2013), the expansion of both international trade and TNCs is to be explained – not by a change in transport costs or trade barriers (so long as these continue to remain relatively low by historical standards) – but by a change in inventory holding costs made possible through ICT-based innovation and the associated organisational innovations, most notably the just-in-time system. While the econometric demonstrations of this have been in terms of intra-firm or intra-TNC trade (using the traditional definition of a firm in ownership terms), and this is still largely necessary for measurement reasons, the underlying explanation applies just as readily to the emergence and growth of global value chains that incorporate various partner or affiliated organisations into the wider international networks of the TNC. All this, of course, reinforces the point that Ietto-Gillies has rightly stressed from my own work, namely, that trade, FDI and contractual partnerships are largely complementary in processes of TNC growth, and indeed they have become ever more so in recent times.

A second observation here is that I doubt whether internalisation theorists would accept Ietto-Gillies's claim that they are at a loss to explain the trend towards externalisation in the last three decades. Casson, in particular, always saw the processes of internalisation or externalisation as entirely symmetrical, moving readily from one to the other as the nature of transaction costs shifted in either or both the market or non-market means of coordination of economic activity (see e.g. Casson, 1979). A large part of the explanation for changes in transaction costs within each mode of coordination would be the kinds of changes in the environment which Ietto-Gillies describes. While it is true that transaction cost economics has tended to focus on manager vs. manager or manager vs. shareholder (principal-agent) conflicts, it can also be applied to manager vs. worker conflicts in traditional class or industrial relations terms – Coase's main original point of reference was the employment contract with a firm. These conflicts can be examined in terms of the scope that exists for rent seeking behaviours within (or beyond) the firm. However, where I do think Ietto-Gillies's argument is well taken in her discussion of these issues is that the relevant transaction costs of alternative modes may be influenced by pro-active management strategies, and not just by an exogenous shift in the environment beyond the control of any individual decision taker. So strategies have co-evolved with the environment, and the move towards externalisation is, in part, deliberately designed to increase the capture of rents by strengthening bargaining positions. These aspects of active management and the pursuit of power (rents), rather than efficiency (profits), are indeed neglected in most transaction cost approaches in the international business field.

However, in considering the extent to which the established theories of the TNC can be equally well adapted to explain either internalisation or externalisation, I do see some greater difficulties with the evolutionary approach to internalisation originally set out by Kogut and Zander (1993), unless that is thoroughly reworked. Their theory depicts the firm as a social community characterised by certain shared values, which encourages and lowers the costs of internal knowledge transfer (relative to external transfer), and hence promotes the internalisation of knowledge development and exchange within the TNC. Yet we now appreciate that social groups or communities (business networks) can often be formed successfully externally as well as internally, as argued at least implicitly above with reference to the new definition of a TNC as a coordinator of international business networks with both internal and external elements. Indeed, contemporary social network analysis has more often adopted such a person-based rather than a strictly organisation-based notion of ties in assessing network relationships. So, while conventional internalisation theory can readily be inverted to become a theory of externalisation, this is not so evidently the case with Kogut and Zander's interpretation of the logic for internalisation in terms of organisational sociology. One can, of course, depict functioning business networks as social groups or communities, but generalising this approach to potentially apply equally to internal or external networks challenges the

Kogut and Zander interpretation of the firm as a kind of privileged social community. If we try and avoid this difficulty by re-defining the TNC (like above) to consist of close social ties rather than the ownership of assets, then it might be objected that we would run into the same sorts of worries over tautology as have plagued the transaction cost version of internalisation theory. The question would become the conditions under which close social ties and shared values come about externally as well as internally. Indeed, once we start down this route there is no reason on the other side of the story to suppose that social ties and shared values always exist or work well internally, especially in large and geographically disparate TNCs. Moreover, as noted earlier, social groups may still contain divergent interests, and so the original Kogut and Zander story tends to downplay the existence of potential intra-group conflicts and rent seeking (on the relevance of which, see Mudambi and Navarra, 2004). These aspects would follow more naturally from transaction cost reasoning, even if these accounts of the existence of the TNC have often been somewhat narrower in character than might have been appropriate (as just discussed above).

I think that Ietto-Gillies and I would agree that the long-term shift from a trend that was predominantly towards internalisation in the 1960s and 1970s to a trend that is predominantly towards externalisation today, has to be seen in terms of an historical evolution in the socio-economic paradigm that characterises the environment for international business. Ietto-Gillies seems to think of this change mainly in terms of the playing out of the conflict between capital and labour, and the interplay between TNCs and states (on which more below). Instead I see the new paradigm more broadly as the emergence of a new system of production, and consequently of the relationships between the actors within it, closer to the notion of paradigm change proposed by Freeman and Louçã (2001) and Perez (2002). The shift from a system of production driven by economies of scale in large plants towards one driven by economies of scope and flexibility in the information age, readily explains the change from internalisation to externalisation. (For a further discussion of these issues and their implications for the TNC, see Cantwell, 2013.) As part of the same process of the fragmentation of production and the fine slicing of the value chain, the nature of work has been transformed and the bargaining strength of trade unions has been weakened. These combined processes of change in the economy and society are reflected in the changing nature of organisational and social structures in the new system of production. However, I would not describe these changes as 'external' (to the firm) – since, as Ietto-Gillies also rightly emphasises, firms and the pursuit of their interests have been an integral or endogenous part of this economic and social change. So it would be more accurate to say that these changes reach well beyond the scope of the firm and its organisational form.

As Ietto-Gillies has correctly observed, as part of this same process of change, labour has become more mobile across firms, across sectors, and across countries. In the previous mass production system a worker might spend an entire lifetime in one type of job, beginning from an apprenticeship, while now the onus is on the individual's capacity to become multi-skilled and to multi-task, which may lead to more varied opportunities for at least some people. The linkages between science and technology, and hence between firms and universities, have steadily risen as technology has become increasingly science- and information-based. As products have become more multi-technology in character, and technological knowledge itself within any field has become more complex, understanding (know-how and know-why) in any area of expertise increasingly requires access to a raft of supporting knowledge beyond the scope of specialists within a given field. This requirement to combine knowledge from more diverse domains necessitates a wider range of formal and informal ties to other firms and universities, and the need to develop a greater capacity to source knowledge internationally.

Turning to the eclectic paradigm or 'ownership, location, and internalisation' (OLI) framework, I think that Ietto-Gillies misses an important distinction between Dunning's concept of ownership advantages and what later were called (by Rugman and others) firm-specific advantages. Ietto-Gillies follows a common belief that ownership advantages and firm-specific advantages are equivalent, which belief I suspect came about around the time that attention shifted in international business scholarship from the country level to the firm level, as I described earlier. Yet both Dunning and Vernon had a notion of TNC capabilities that incorporated some collective elements in their home country of origin. The term 'ownership advantages' is the shortened version of what Dunning had called the 'advantages of the nationality of ownership'. In other words, he intended to refer not to the ownership of assets (another common mistake) but to the advantages associated with having emanated from some specific home country. These would therefore include capabilities accessed through inter-organisational networks in the home country, and access to home country institutions, as well as capabilities held in-house in the TNC itself (firm-specific advantages). While in the internalisation era there seemed little need to emphasise this distinction, in the contemporary period of externalisation Dunning's distinction becomes ever more vital and prescient, since capabilities are held in business networks and not just in in-house facilities. Likewise, location advantages are not just host country advantages, but refer to resources and capabilities associated with any unit of observation of a host location, as appropriate to the context examined – sometimes a sub-national region, or a cross-national region like the EU. I will come back to this issue in considering Ietto-Gillies's discussion of the role of the nation state in international business below.

Another aspect of the eclectic paradigm that I think is worth emphasising is its flexibility and adaptability. This means that the way in which the eclectic paradigm has been interpreted and used over time has changed, and indeed has undergone more than one transformation as it has evolved (see e.g. Eden and Dai, 2010). Critics of the eclectic paradigm have often seen this versatility of the eclectic paradigm and its theoretical openness as a weakness, but in my view it has actually been its greatest strength and the reason for its continued centrality in the international business field. Originally, the chief objective of the eclectic paradigm was to provide a synthesis of the various economic theories of international business, and a framework within which they could be compared on some common ground where they offered genuinely competing explanations of a common phenomenon. Although it was probably unanticipated at the time, the eclectic paradigm is sufficiently general in nature that it has continued to fulfil a similar function but now in a broader analytical context as the domain of international business theory has expanded. Today, the eclectic paradigm offers a template for incorporating and relating a wider range of multidisciplinary perspectives and theories on the subject. It serves as the analytical means by which the field is still brought together and becomes more than just the sum of its various disciplinary parts. I am sure that this is a development that would have made Dunning very contented, since he placed great store on shifting the field of international business in a more interdisciplinary direction (Dunning, 1989).

Finally, I come to Ietto-Gillies's remarks on the role of nation states, which rightly call our attention to the need to re-introduce the political science dimension into the multidisciplinary mix that constitutes our current thinking on TNCs, which has been relatively neglected since the time of Vernon (1971) – although those such as Dunning or Kobrin had been writing especially on governments and international business, and the role of public policies. Recent work by those like Henisz, Makhija or Cuervo-Cazurra has been linking TNC strategies to their interactions with governments and political structures, which has dovetailed quite nicely with more sociologically-grounded work on institutions and international business. So in one sense I suspect that Ietto-Gillies is here pushing at an open door into a branch of international business theory development in which a process of revival seems to be already under way and which is likely to draw in further research interest in the near future.

However, although it is certainly true that the borders between countries are political boundaries, I do think that it oversimplifies matters from an international business perspective to think of the crossing of borders by the TNC merely in terms of encountering a different governmental, regulatory and policy regime. Countries and regions of the world have been separated by the barriers of geographical distance for so long in history, that the constraints of distance have only gradually begun to diminish over the past few hundred years, and especially since the transport and communications revolutions of the mid-19th century which Ietto-Gillies mentions. From this longer-term perspective, the emergence and growth of nation states in this same historical epoch since the Middle Ages is a reflection of these – by now inherited – human and cultural boundaries, rather than the reason for them. What those of us also in the innovation studies field call national systems of innovation are differentiated not just because the system of government and regulatory structures are distinct, but because of a range of other associated formal institutions, and an even more complex set of informal institutions or ways of doing business. The connections between firms, and between firms and non-firm actors vary greatly across countries, and not just for the reasons of the specificities of government policy and regulation. It can be argued e.g. that the reason inward FDI penetration in Japan is so low for its level of economic development has little to do with formal barriers or regulatory constraints on foreign enterprise, but rather with distinctive ways of doing business and forming inter-organisational network relationships that are often misunderstood or misinterpreted by Western firms. Moreover, as alluded to in passing earlier, once we mention national systems of innovation we come naturally as well to the role of regional systems of innovation, both at the sub-national level and at the supra-national level. While each of these levels of regional entity also has its administrative authority structures, they too are not fully described as locational units by these political and regulatory features. So although Ietto-Gillies is certainly right to ask us to bring the role of states more into our discourse, in my view it overstates matters to say that this is the only aspect of locational variety encountered by TNCs which is not experienced also by purely domestic firms. As geographical distance rises, so does institutional variety and differences.

When Ietto-Gillies speaks of the advantages that TNCs have in their negotiations with nation states, owing to their greater degree of centralised power to move resources across global space, I believe she describes best the situation for the finance function, which is one aspect of the system of production that has also been caught up in the effects of socio-economic paradigm change mentioned earlier (see Perez, 2002). Thus, there are contemporary debates over whether governments can find a way of effectively taxing TNCs where they have most of their productive activities and their sales, and of curbing the use of offshore financial centres that offer low or zero tax rates. However, nation states are in a relatively stronger position when it comes to the regulation of markets and competition – at least in larger countries, and when it comes to access to knowledge and skills – states have more leverage everywhere. Indeed, TNCs may suffer from regulatory confusion or inter-country disagreements, where there are competing authorities with claims, e.g. in the case of mergers and acquisitions (M&As) that are approved in the US but not in the EU, or vice versa. As well as the benefits of globally dispersing their value chain activities, this has also led to an increased vulnerability to global risks for TNCs, in the case of a natural or environmental disaster or a major civil or political disturbance in any part of a global supply chain.

Rather than seeing matters simply in terms of the degree of bargaining power that nation states can exercise in extracting rents from TNCs (although I understand the point about all actors contributing fairly to the tax base of a country), we might ask more generally under what conditions countries can benefit from globalisation, just as TNCs do. I would suggest that a virtuous circle may be created where they cultivate some centres of specialised skills and knowledge in a locally differentiated field of expertise; these centres then exchange knowledge globally with poles of suitably complementary capabilities elsewhere. This is how contemporary global cities have been revitalised or emerged, drawing upon a variety of economic and business ties with other such cities. The form of institutional environment that is most conducive to such internationally interconnected, but locally specialised, growth might be described as a relatively open society, rather than a relatively closed one. Once again this openness refers to a wide variety of formal and informal institutions that characterise a society, so what I mean by openness is very far from being reducible (say) to a country's trade and FDI regime. It is above all an openness to new knowledge and ideas, from outside as well as from within. In this context, we should not see cultural and institutional diversity across countries as a barrier to be overcome, but rather as a rich source of diversity, the combination of which can generate advantages both for TNCs and countries. It should be further noted that for TNCs to take advantage of such cross-border diversity, they require decentralised and distributed organisational structures, rather than the centralised direction of resources that may apply with respect to the finance function. This logic of organisational decentralisation is a critical part of the current trend towards externalisation emphasised earlier. I might add that, as quite rightly argued by Shenkar (2001), 'cultural distance' is a misleading concept. The commonly used measures of this construct are even more misleading, not least as the liabilities of foreignness are not symmetrical – it is often easier to move in one direction than the other, meaning a substantial disparity between inward and outward FDI. To take advantage of international variety, TNCs need to learn about the distinct ways of doing business in each location, and this requires them to become locally embedded and to build up the status of a local insider in business networks.

Therefore, I would argue that TNCs need to be understood, not just in the context of nation states, but more generally in the context of locational diversity of various kinds (including differences in political and regulatory environments), in which the degree of locational diversity across countries is of a qualitatively different order of magnitude to that experienced by domestic firms, even in a large country. For international business and, in particular, for the innovative TNC, the main reason why this matters is due to the far greater diversity in the settings encountered for interaction with local capabilities across locations, and in the distinct nature of those locally differentiated capabilities. Operating in such a diverse set of environments, in different national systems of innovation, provides TNCs with the opportunity to create more diverse kinds of knowledge, and to discover a much broader range of new combinations of knowledge. This brings us back to my earlier discussion of the change in the nature of the TNC itself as an actor, since TNCs are distinguished from other firms by what Kogut and Zander (1993) called their combinative capabilities. These have gradually enabled TNCs to serve increasingly as system integrators across international networks that connect a series of other actors, each with very different kinds of knowledge and capabilities. So, as Ietto-Gillies rightly remarks, our notion of TNC strategy should not be confined to rivalrous interactions with others, but must increasingly recognise and emphasise strategies with respect to cooperative relationships in local and international business networks (including those with non-firm actors). As she suggests, these may, in turn, be a major source of advantages relative to a TNC's major competitors.

References

Cantwell, J.A. (2013), 'Blurred boundaries between firms, and new boundaries within (large multinational) firms: the impact of decentralized networks for innovation', *Seoul Journal of Economics*, 26(1), 1-32.

Casson, M.C. (1979), *Alternatives to the Multinational Enterprise*, London: Macmillan.

Cowling, K. and Sugden, R. (1987), *Transnational Monopoly Capitalism*, Brighton: Wheatsheaf.

Dunning, J.H. (1989), 'The study of international business: a plea for a more interdisciplinary approach', *Journal of International Business Studies*, 20(3), 411-436.

Dunning, J.H. and Lundan, S.M. (2008), *Multinational Enterprises and the Global Economy*, second edition, Cheltenham: Edward Elgar.

Eden, L. and Dai, L. (2010), 'Rethinking the O in Dunning's OLI/eclectic paradigm', *Multinational Business Review*, 18(2), 13-34.

Feinberg, S.E. and Keane, M.P. (2006), 'Accounting for the growth of MNC-based trade using a structural model of U.S. MNCs', *American Economic Review*, 96(5), 1515-1558.

Freeman, C. and Louçã, F. (2001), *As Time Goes By: From the Industrial Revolutions to the Information Revolution*, Oxford: Oxford University Press.

Iammarino, S. and McCann, P. (2013), *Multinationals and Economic Geography: Location, Technology and Innovation*, Cheltenham: Edward Elgar.

Ietto-Gillies, G. (2012), *Transnational Corporations and International Production: Trends, Theories, Effects*, Cheltenham: Edward Elgar.

Kogut, B. and Zander, U. (1993), 'Knowledge of the firm and the evolutionary theory of the multinational corporation', *Journal of International Business Studies*, 24(4), 625-645.

Mudambi, R. and Navarra, P. (2004), 'Is knowledge power? Knowledge flows, subsidiary power and rent-seeking within MNCs', *Journal of International Business Studies*, 35(5), 385-406.

Nelson, R.R. (1998), 'The agenda for growth theory: a different point of view', *Cambridge Journal of Economics*, 22(4), 497-520.

Perez, C. (2002), *Technological Revolutions and Financial Capital: The Dynamics of Bubbles and Golden Ages*, Cheltenham: Elgar.

Shenkar, O. (2001), 'Cultural distance revisted: towards a more rigorous conceptualization and measurement of cultural differences', *Journal of International Business Studies*, 32(3), 519-535.

Vernon, R. (1971), *Sovereignty at Bay: The Multinational Spread of U.S. Enterprises*, New York: Basic Books.

SUGGESTED CITATION:

Cantwell, J.A. (2014) 'A commentary on Grazia Ietto-Gillies' paper: "The Theory of the Transnational Corporation at 50+"'. *Economic Thought*, 3.2, pp. 58-66.
http://www.worldeconomicsassociation.org/files/journals/economicthought/WEA-ET-3-2-Cantwell.pdf

Reply to John Cantwell's Commentary on Grazia Ietto-Gillies' paper: 'The Theory of the Transnational Corporation at 50+'

Grazia Ietto-Gillies, London South Bank University and Birkbeck University of London, UK
iettogg@lsbu.ac.uk

Keywords: transnational corporations, Hymer; Vernon, internalisation theory, Dunning, Cantwell, Kogut and Zander, nation-states and transnationals, history of economic ideas

My thanks to John Cantwell for taking the trouble to read carefully and respond to my paper *The Theory of the Transnational Corporation at 50+*. These comments greatly add to my contribution by deepening the discourse. Here I take the opportunity to add some comments and clarifications to those of John Cantwell.

Cantwell starts his comments with very interesting methodological remarks about the trajectory of the international business (IB) literature after its starting point from – or very closely to – economics. I very much agree with him on the positive role played by multi- and inter-disciplinarity in the development of the subject. Indeed, I would go further in saying that these developments need not be specific to IB only. I believe that other parts of economics would greatly benefit from liaisons with other disciplines – particularly sociological and political sciences. They would also benefit from more grounded links with empirics and from the use of a wider variety of methodologies.

We both agree that the trends towards externalisation need new approaches to the firm and particularly to the TNC. Dunning and Lundan's (2008) work is a good example of authors aware that old approaches may no longer suffice. Years ago, Cowling and Sugden (1987, p. 12) saw the need for a redefinition of the firm and the TNC on the basis of their control over units which are external in terms of ownership but are nonetheless dependent on the principal firm. They give the following definitions: 'A firm is the means of coordinating production from one center of strategic decision-making. A transnational is the means of coordinating production from one center of strategic decision-making when this coordination takes a firm across national boundaries.' This part of their work was further developed in their 1998 article.

I agree with Cantwell that the proponents of the Internalisation Theory saw as symmetrical the process of internalisation versus externalisation. After all, in a static sense, internalisation implies that, at the micro level, there is another choice and there always was. However, my criticism stems from historical developments at the macro level. Yes, managers always had the choice between growth via internal activities or via external ones such as licensing or sub-contracting. But the fact remains that, historically, there was a tendency towards internalisation up to the early 1970s (and this, in my view, helps to explain why the theory was developed at that point in time). However, the trend was reversed dramatically from the 1980s onwards. Given that the managers were always faced with the same choices, how do we explain the two different trends? In my view they can only be explained by bringing in external socio-political elements. The increased internalisation, combined with other socio-economic factors, led to a more powerful workforce in the late 1960s and early 1970s. As a reaction to this, firms, and indeed public institutions, moved towards subcontracting and other externalisation modalities. This contributed to weaken the bargaining power of labour as we see today. In other words, the internalisation theory can explain the choice between situations in which externalisation may be preferred to internalisation (or *vice versa*), at the micro level. However, my point is that we need a theory that explains both micro and macro level patterns, as well as the historical trends, and how the macro and micro levels affect each other. This is a key example in which we need to analyse the links between micro and macro levels as well as use interdisciplinarity - two issues Cantwell emphasises in his comments. I would add the emphasis that historical trends help to clarify the interrelationships between the micro and macro levels.

In discussing internalisation, Cantwell introduces some poignant comments on Kogut and Zander's (1993) evolutionary theory. I would, once again, like to use external, historical trends to further support Cantwell's point. The political and economic contexts of the last three decades have brought about several changes, including the following two related to both the private and public sectors. First, labour has become more mobile in two different meanings. The gradual erosion of secure and stable employment contracts means that labour has become more mobile across firms and sectors. It has also become more mobile across countries, which is one of the characteristics of globalisation. As skilled labourers move across institutions, sectors or countries, they form wider networks. Second, universities and public research centres have been told for years that a measure of their success is the ability to forge links with private producers. Whether this is conducive to better research or not, the fact is that, increasingly, companies' skilled labour has the opportunity of networking with public researchers. All this points to the increasing relevance of networks that span outside the boundaries of the firm. Thus Kogut and Zander's idea of the firm as the hub of exclusive, privileged networks may be undermined by the empirics of historical trends.

One last point I would like to make refers to the role of nation-states in my approach to the explanation of TNCs' strategies and activities. Yes, the nation-state and the role of governments have often been included in IB writings: from Hymer post-dissertation work to Vernon to Dunning. In more recent writings the emphasis on policies of attractiveness (of inward FDI) necessarily implies a role for the state and its government. However, my point is not so much about policies of single states and the politics behind them – important though these are. The key point in my discourse is the fact the actors that can plan, organise and control across frontiers – as the TNCs can – have a bargaining advantage when dealing with actors who cannot do so, or not to the same extent. Thus the ex-ante contractual power of TNCs is considerably stronger than that of the workforce they confront in each country or of governments that try to outbid each other in sweeteners or suppliers who are often location bound. It is multinationality *per se* that gives advantages to the TNCs. The bargaining power over these three sets of actors can be turned into market power. There can also be further advantages of multinationality – including risk spreading and learning from the diverse innovation environments of different nation states. The latter is a field to which Cantwell has made a major contribution. For these reasons the theory of the TNC cannot be just an extension of the theory of the firm in general, or of the big firm in particular. The different regulatory regimes of nation-states lead to situations that require a qualitatively different approach from the traditional theory of the firm. The stress on advantages of multinationality has policy implications: for the labour movement it implies building bridges across frontiers and avoiding the games of setting Poles against Italians or British against Romanians. The other relevant policy implication may be related to separatist movements which are springing up everywhere be it Scotland, Northern Italy or Catalonia. While devolution of some powers from the centre may be in the interest of regions and countries, the main beneficiaries of full separation may end up being the TNCs as they will have more policy centres – i.e. more nation-states – in competition with each other. I recently read in the British press that one of the pledges of the aspiring separate Scotland will be to lower corporation tax in competition with the one – already quite low – of Britain.

Cantwell points out the role of cultural differences as well as the relevance of local and regional characteristics for TNCs' strategic decisions. I do not consider them in the paper under discussion, though there is a small role for cultural differences between nation-states and for regional variation in regulatory regimes in the relevant chapter in my book (Ietto-Gillies, 2012, ch. 14). I agree that cultural issues should play a bigger role. However, the tremendous increase in cross-country FDI in the last few decades is testimony that cultural barriers can be overcome. Inward FDI into Japan may have been constrained by cultural factors; however, had other conditions been favourable – such as government policies – the cultural barriers would have been overcome. Cultural distance is only part of the story. After all, Japanese companies coming from a different culture managed to overcome the barriers and successfully expand their FDI abroad. Why could not Western companies overcome the cultural distance – if that had been the only or main problem – and invest in Japan? After all cultural barriers have largely been overcome by Western TNCs investing in China. Cultural barriers can often be overcome by joint ventures, a modality of internationalisation more appealing to host countries, as well as of help to the foreign firm in learning about a new cultural and institutional environment.

Finally, I should say that I am pleased to see that my comments above have been fully considered in the final revised version of Cantwell's Commentary. This process has led to further interesting points by Cantwell on: the network firm; the drivers of externalisation; the advantages and disadvantages of nation-states *vis-à-vis* the TNCs. Our exchange has widened the debate beyond my original paper and has led to convergence of views on many points.

Additional References

Cowling, K. and Sugden, R. (1987) *Transnational Monopoly Capitalism*, Brighton: Wheatsheaf.

Cowling, K. and Sugden, R. (1998) 'The essence of the modern corporation: markets, strategic decision-making and the theory of the firm', *The Manchester School*, 66 (1), 59–86.

Ietto-Gillies, G. (2012) *Transnational Corporations and International Production. Trends, Theories, Effects*, 2nd edition, Cheltenham, UK and Northampton, MA, USA: Edward Elgar.

SUGGESTED CITATION:

Ietto-Gillies, G. (2014) 'Reply to John Cantwell's Commentary on Grazia Ietto-Gillies' paper: "The Theory of the Transnational Corporation at 50+"'. *Economic Thought*, 3.2, pp. 67-69.
http://www.worldeconomicsassociation.org/files/journals/economicthought/WEA-ET-3-2-Ietto-Gillies-Reply.pdf

If 'Well-Being' is the Key Concept in Political Economy…

Claudio Gnesutta[1], Faculty of Economics, La Sapienza University of Rome, Italy
claudio.gnesutta@uniroma1.it

Abstract

If 'well-being' is to be the key concept in political economy, then economists are placed, from a methodological viewpoint, in an uncomfortable position. A well-being approach requires consideration of several non-economic dimensions strongly interrelated with the economic process, and failure to consider them means that the subsequent economic analysis cannot be based on steadily defined categories and, therefore, economists cannot value the full implications of their policy prescriptions. In this note, I show how an interrelated economic-social scheme able to analyse (sustainable) well-being calls for a broadening of the range of social factors interacting (in short and long term) with the market equilibria, and that this entails both new analytical categories and a new socio-economic relations model; in the absence of this apparatus, the effects of economic policies on society are not reliable and, therefore, ought to be systematically subject to a 'precaution principle'.

Keywords: well-being, GDP measurement, social accounting, economic policy, economic and social progress

JEL classification: I31, B41, E01, E02, E51

1. Why the Consideration of 'Well-Being' Produces a Problem

For a long time, interpretations of the economic situation and economic policy prescriptions have referred to an aggregate – the Gross Domestic Product – as an appropriate picture of the community's welfare and gauge of society's civil progress. In

---

[1] Claudio Gnesutta is retired full professor in the Dipartimento di Economia Pubblica at the La Sapienza, Università di Roma (Italy).

recent times, the belief has increased – even outside the world of scholars – that such an aggregate, as a valuation of market production, cannot also be a measure of how well-off people are.[2] If the economists' reference should indeed be welfare – however defined – rather than product (in the broad sense of GDP), then a radical change of viewpoint is called for, almost a new paradigm, raising a key analytical question.

With reference to the long debate on the need to shift attention from a production-oriented view to a broader view of social progress, the SSF Report[3] has identified well-being in a context of sustainability, as the most appropriate indicator for a non-misleading evaluation of economic processes and related policies. This proposal aims to redefine the structure of economic categories, at present centred on the 'product', to a structure centred on 'sustainable well-being'. But this means changing the present view of the economic process, since it changes the object of what constitutes the 'value' resulting from the social process. Innovation with regard to the central category of political economy transforms the contents of the aggregates actually used and so also the economists' agenda – at both the analytical level and that of economic policy interventions.

With this paper, I intend to submit for discussion my conviction that the issue entails, not only the need to re-define and re-build a more meaningful economic indicator, but also to question the entire economic conceptual apparatus. From this point of view it is worth recalling that the economy became an object of scientific investigation when scholars established as the (remarkable) object of their research, the aggregate outcomes of the interrelated individual behaviours in a restricted system of market exchange. It is also worth remembering that the production of well-being can be interpreted by (market and non-market) exchanges, and that this means shifting the focus onto the aggregate outcomes of interrelated behaviours in a social space not restricted to the market.

But refocusing research in this macroeconomic direction means – and this is my conclusion – that economists place themselves in an uncomfortable position in which they cannot count on clearly defined categories; therefore, they are forced to work with an inevitably inadequate and partial macroeconomic framework without any guarantee that their economic policy prescriptions are well-founded, reference being made only to a

---

[2] The critique of GDP as an indicator of well-being is borne out by the institutional commitment to build new welfare indicators, for example with the EU Beyond GDP initiative and its Italian BES Report (ISTAT 2013). For a more general examination of alternatives to GDP able to provide a measure of individual and collective well-being, see Fleurbaey 2009.

[3] Stiglitz, Sen, Fitoussi (2009). I refer to this report (hereafter SSF) because the authors' proposal to adopt the concept of 'sustainable well-being' poses the question in all its complexity. In fact, their search for a better economic indicator concerns the macroeconomic dimension and involves not only the flow of well-being but also the stock of well-being productive resources associated with long-term sustainability.

concept of economic efficiency more narrow than a concept of social well-being.[4]

To support my thesis, I refer, for the sake of convenience, to the SSF Commission's proposal, which recognises 'sustainable well-being' as the crucial category required for an adequate view of the economic process.[5] In sections 2 and 3, I present, in general terms, the contents of 'well-being' and of 'productive resources of well-being', both critical SSF-concepts[6], and compare them with the respective content of 'product' and 'capital' categories at the core of current economic analysis. By replacing product with well-being I am able (in section 4) to provide, using a social accounting scheme, a representation of the economic process through which, reinterpreting the different meanings of the resulting network of aggregates, I show (section 5) that a representation of the macroeconomic system centred on quality of life drives economic analysis to new ground, to a different view of the process of production of 'value' – and towards an analytical view of society – that should stimulate, in accordance with the hope of the Report, economists' interest in 'a discussion of societal values, for what we, as a society, care about, and whether we are really striving for what is important' (Stiglitz, Sen, Fitoussi, 2009, p. 18).

2. The New 'Production Boundaries': From 'Product' to 'Well-Being'...

The value production concept is central for economic analysis. As we know, the current concept of 'product' (in terms of GDP and related aggregates) is basically an expression of market production, and a legacy of understanding needs related, in the forties and fifties, to anti-cyclical analysis and policies. On the other hand, and as is equally well-known, market production is not the only component of the current product aggregate; given the importance assumed by the public sector, it also includes the provision of non-market public services.

---

[4] In another article on the SSF, I concluded that the researchers' proposal provides a dramatic challenge for economic analysis and policy; in fact, in the present situation, '(t)he economist (and the economic policy authorities) are (...) in a dilemma between working with a *restricted* (to economic values) representation inevitably *partial*, or working on the basis of an *extended* representation empirically *undefined*'. (Gnesutta, 2013).

[5] 'The report distinguishes between an assessment of current well-being and an assessment of sustainability, whether this can last over time. Current well-being has to do with both economic resources, such as income, and with non-economic aspects of peoples' life (what they do and what they can do, how they feel, and the natural environment they live in). Whether these levels of well-being can be sustained over time depends on whether stocks of capital that matter for our lives (natural, physical, human, social) are passed on to future generations' (Stiglitz, Sen, Fitoussi, 2009, p. 11). Although complementary, the two analytical categories of well-being and its sustainability are '*examined separately*' (Stiglitz, Sen, Fitoussi, 2009, p. 17, p. 61, p. 77).

[6] The exclusive reference to SSF concepts is not intended to sideline all other contributors to the debate on well-being, fairness and happiness. In this note the question at issue does not concern the content of the categories, but the methodological aspect of their consideration in the (socio-)economic process.

The well-being concept refers instead to 'a rich array of attributes – such as belonging, fulfilment, self-image, autonomy, feelings, and the attitudes of others – that are associated with Quality of Life. (...) Human well-being depends on what resources enable people to do and to be, and the ability to convert resources into a good life' (Stiglitz, Sen, Fitoussi, 2009, p. 144). This concept of well-being comprises not only the 'economic' dimension, but also includes features normally attributed, widely if not universally, to other 'social' dimensions. Whatever the definition may be, the concept of well-being is inevitably multidimensional; in fact, the Commission's interpretation of well-being is characterised by eight simultaneous dimensions: in addition to (i) material living standards, closely related to the current economic concept of the product, it proposes consideration of the conditions of (ii) health; (iii) education; (iv) personal activities; including work; (v) political voice and governance; (vi) social connections and relationships; (vii) environment (present and future); (viii) insecurity, of an economic as well as a physical nature (see Stiglitz, Sen, Fitoussi, 2009, pp. 14-16).

Table 1: The production boundaries of well-being flow

	Market productive activities	Market goods and services	**PRODUCT**
WELL-BEING	Public services production	Non-market goods and services	
	'Other' productive activities of well-being		

All these activities affect the quality of life and contribute to people's well-being.[7] As can be seen in Table 1, the indications relating to some of them are also part of the concept of product currently in use: not only most of the production of goods[8] supplied in the market, but also, as pointed out above, most of the public services. However, the proposed well-being concept requires a careful choice among the many activities for personal and

---

[7] As the product is a macroeconomic concept, well-being is here dealt with also as a macroeconomic aggregate. That is to say, here I am not interested in the (important) question of how to represent the individual (subjective) feeling of well-being, but in considering a framework from an objective point of view, since how society is organised makes a difference for people's lives.

[8] As has been well-known since publication of the classic and seminal Nordhaus-Tobin (1973) paper, there are goods and services that – as we shall see later – are traded in the market, and included in the GDP, that do not offer any contribution to well-being.

collective life that makes these two concepts incommensurable.[9]

So, the value of the current product is only a part of the flow of well-being in a given period; and whether it is a great or a small part is a secondary issue in the present case. The relevant issue is that the consideration of a sector of 'other' productive activities of well-being is vital to understanding the structure of the economic process, since to make explicit the institutional distinction between market and non-market means, from an analytical point of view, sets the world of capitalist social relations counter to the systems of other social norms.

3. ... And From 'Capital' Stock To 'Well-Being Productive Resources' Stock

The other innovative aspect of the SSF's proposal is the reference to a concept of 'sustainability' of well-being over time. Well-being measured at a point in time makes little sense since it is a moment in a continuous process, the current effects of which influence, progressively or regressively, the future. In fact, also in the measurement of standard of living, it is not only the current income flows that are important, but in addition the consumption opportunities over time.[10] Granted that well-being is to be seen in a context of sustainability, we must take the future into account. But the production of future well-being is based upon the future resources – the availability of which depends on present behaviours. So, if the current process of consumption affects the conditions for future (well-being) production, then it is necessary that in the present production and consumption processes the stocks of available productive resources are not depleted. The only way to guarantee the sustainability process is to leave 'to future generations (...) enough resources of all kinds to provide them with opportunity sets at least as large as the ones we have had for ourselves' (Stiglitz, Sen, Fitoussi, 2009, p.250).

It is therefore essential to state precisely the form of (well-being) productive resources. In current national accounting the production of resources to be used for future production is essentially a matter of man-made capital goods embedded in firm activity, or in civil construction and public infrastructures. In the SSF's proposal, by contrast, the 'resources' taken into account are manifold: 'fossil resources, renewables other environmental resources, but also physical, human and social capital, or general knowledge' (see Stiglitz, Sen, Fitoussi, 2009, p. 250, pp. 265-66).

---

[9] It suffices to point out that the difference between product and well-being derives from important aspects of economic and social life: household self-consumption, leisure, use of common goods, collective services (security, medical, educational, housing facilities, sport facilities and so on).
[10] On the limits of SSF proposals see the ample survey of Vanoli 2010.

Claudio Gnesutta

Table 2: Stock of well-being productive resources

	Man-made capital	Capital
Well-being productive resources	Human resources	
	Social resources	
	Natural resources	

As can be seen in Table 2, the range of factors governing economic and social progress is greatly extended when it includes, within the boundaries delimiting the stock of well-being productive resources, not only (man-made) capital goods privately owned or subject to market forces, but also the collective assets managed outside the market and embedded in personal ability, social relations and natural conditions. The preservation, or better, the further accumulation, of these resources ensures opportunities for future well-being.

4. The Sustainable Well-Being Production Process: The Structure Of Relations ...

Taking into consideration an economic process centred on well-being, and especially on sustainable well-being, means interpreting society's reproduction from a different viewpoint. In this context, the production process does not refer solely to goods and services to be exchanged on the market ('market-goods'), but also to the other goods and services that generate well-being without passing through the market (here defined as 'value-goods'); moreover, resources productive of well-being are also the result of a production process.[11] Therefore, there are three interdependent production lines, since value-goods are produced with the use of market-goods, too, and the production of these requires the use of value-goods; the reproduction of resources necessary to the overall production entails the use of both market-goods and value-goods. In essence, the process of production of well-being is a process of production of market-goods, value-goods and resources by means of market-goods, value-goods and resources. The goal of

---

[11] My use of a market-goods concept restricted to capitalist exchange relationships is intend to separate sharply market-goods from value-goods activities. In this way, the boundaries of the two sectors are neat and the accounting relations network highlights all the 'class of events' that the economist ought to take into account when explaining the social process.

98

this depiction is to define the socio-economic macro-structure that determines the 'objective' conditions for the production of those value goods – the availability of which allows the individual to ensure his own 'subjective' well-being.

Description of the (sustainable) well-being production process amounts to constructing an appropriate list of inputs – market and non-market, including the consumption of (different) resources – necessary to obtain the several outputs. In order to produce, for example, the value-goods – care and assistance, educational, political and social security and so on – procedures and institutions are necessary that employ resources and (market and non-market) goods and services. Even the reproduction of productive resources – liable to depreciation and depletion through the production process itself or other events – derives from institutionally organised activities with the task of restoring or extending human capabilities, social relationships and the natural environment.

To attribute to the production concept a different content from the usual, involves redefining the content of the entire system of income, consumption and capital formation aggregates: in other words of the entire network of macroeconomic relationships. Matrix 1, applying the usual tools of social accounting[12], reconstructs the structure of this network, albeit in very simplified form; it takes into account two sectors of productive activity, respectively market-goods and value-goods; one sector of consumption; two areas for the accumulation of productive resources, respectively 'capital' (firm capital goods) and 'HES resources' (other sources productive of well-being, such as human, social and natural resources).[13]

---

[12] Reference is to social accounting of the SNA tradition along the Stone, Stuvel, Ruggles and Ruggles research lines (Eisner 1988) and popularised in Gnesutta (1983).

[13] In this simplified representation the institutions are basically two, one for production and one for consumption. The productive institutions are distinguished between those producing market-goods (firms, subscript $_M$) and those producing value-goods (households, hospitals, schools, universities etc., subscript $_V$); both produce for the consumption and formation of the two types of productive resources (capital K) and HES resources (Z) . For the sake of further simplicity, the production of public services is not distinguished from the production of other value-goods. The activity of consumption is attributed to a single institution, the overall population (subscript $_H$) which also owns the entire final stock of productive resources (wealth R). Surprisingly, a representation of the economic system which aims to analyse a capitalist society doesn't divide the consumption (and wealth) sphere (at the very least) between wage and capital income earners. In fact, the reductive decision to treat social and economic reality as a single institution – the overall population – entails the impossibility of considering significant aspects such as the interdependence of the various lines of production of value-goods and inequality in distribution in income and resources. This can be justified, if at all, only for explanatory convenience: to introduce also only that simple breakdown would increase the matrix boxes from 81 to 144, with greater difficulties in reading the relevant phenomena. If this consideration led me to build an accounting model reduced to the essentials, it does not mean that for the theoretical analysis and for real process interpretation a suitable breakdown by social class or interest groups is not fundamental.

Matrix 1: The (socio-)economic system: market and value goods; capital and HES resources

Matrix 1	Resources Initial stocks (A)	Production Market goods (B)	Value good (C)	Consumption (D)	Resources formation Wealth (E)	Firm's capital (F)	HES Resources (G)	Resources Revaluation (H)	Final stocks (I)	Total
1. Wealth-Resources: Initial stocks						K_H^i	Z_H^i			$K_H^i + Z_H^i$
2. Production: market goods			B_{VM}	C_M		GI_M^K	GI_M^Z			T_M
3. Production: value goods		B_{MV}		C_V		GI_V^K	GI_V^Z			T_V
4. Consumption		Y_M	Y_V							Y_H
5. Wealth accumulation	R_H^i			S_H				$RV(R_H)$		R_H^f
6. Firm's capital formation		D_M^K							K_H^f	$K_H^f + D^K$
7. HES resources formation		D_M^Z	D_V^Z						Z_H^f	$Z_H^f + D^Z$
8. Wealth-resources: revaluation						$RV(K_H)$	$RV(Z_H)$			$Rv(K_H)+ RV(Z_H)$
9. Wealth-Resources: Final stocks					R_H^f					R_H^f
Total	R_H^i	T_M	T_V	Y_H	R_H^f	$K_H^f + D^K$	$Z_H^f + D^Z$	$Rv(R_H)$	$K_H^f + Z_H^f$	

In comparison with the usual accounting schemes, analysis of Matrix 1[14] highlights, from an accounting point of view, the more interesting issues. As regards the production of market-goods (row 2, column B of the Matrix)[15] we may note that:

---

[14] In the Appendix are listed the accounting identities and all the symbols.
[15] Appendix, Identity 2B.

- the 'costs' of market-good production include, as intermediate goods, the part of value-goods (B_{MV}) including all those services currently produced by the social system (directly or by the public sector) that, not exchanged in monetary terms, determine the productive environment in which businesses operate: in particular, the social relations and collective action (justice, crime fighting and prevention, educational programmes and so on) that influence the climate of cooperation and mutual trust and favour firm activity;
- the 'costs' of market-good production include depreciation of the human, social and environmental resources due to the production process (D^Z_M), such as environmental pollution, deterioration of working conditions, the social insecurity of the productive organisation;
- part of the market-good output is used to rebuild both the firm's productive capital (GI^K_M) and the HES resources (GI^Z_M). This is a gross expenditure that offsets, completely or partially, the depreciation of both stock due to market-good production; the expenditure includes 'defensive expenditures', as in the case in which health and education expenses are considered as investments in human capital or remediation of pollution as investment to improve or maintain environmental quality;
- the consumption of market-goods regards only their direct consumption by the population (C_M), while if the market-goods are purchased to be transformed, for example in domestic production, they appear as intermediate goods (B_{MV}) for the production of value-goods.[16]

Similar considerations can be formulated for value-good production (row 3, column C of the Matrix).[17] In addition to the two items (the intermediate goods B_{VM} and B_{MV}) examined above, we may note that:

- human, social and environmental resources also deteriorate in the production of value-goods (D^Z_V);
- part of value-good output is allocated for the reconstruction of both the firm's productive capital (GI^K_V) and the HES resources (GI^Z_V); non-market activities also contribute to defensive consumptions[18];
- the consumption of value-goods (C_V) also comprises, as noted above, the

---

[16] B_{MV} also includes all those expenses incurred in order to participate in the production process (such as the cost of commute to work), but which do not enhance the well-being of people.
[17] Appendix, Identity 3C.
[18] In fact, many expenses are not considered consumption since they are costs to remediate undesirable conditions due to the deterioration of resources (e.g. the effects of pollution, urban traffic, insecurity etc.).

market-goods purchased and transformed by non-firm institutions (for example, meals at home, commuting to work, family care in domestic production, as well as the soup kitchens and assistance services of voluntary work);

- the added value of value-good production indicates the social value produced by non-firm institutions and so the (non-market, non-monetary) income due to those operating in this activity (in the above examples, the home and voluntary workers).

From an economic and political point of view, each box of Matrix1 identifies 'one' socio-economic 'class of events' corresponding to that specific functional (production, consumption and resource formation) and institutional (market and non-market) combination. Identifying the typical transactions forming them is a primary objective and it is not a trivial question: a 'new' representation of the economic process necessarily implies a different content of events internal to each box. For a given well-being concept, the transactions that should be allocated in the aggregates of each box should be identified in a coherent and exhaustive manner. For example, it must be defined (also conventionally) what it is regarded as, and only as, well-being consumption (C_V), what as intermediate goods in market goods production (B_{MV}), what as formation of HES resources (GI^Z_V) and so on. The Matrix should be used as a tool for screening the contents of the old and new classes of relevant 'events' for the economic analysis, and this was the experience of the GDP processing. Of course, the recategorisation and the subsequent network redefinition are a first step in elaborating a model able to explain the socio-economic process; they are a necessary, but not sufficient, condition for any subsequent theoretical explanation and historical interpretation of the society dynamics.[19]

It has already been noted (see note 18) that the matrix does not contain an explicit treatment of the distributive processes, essential for assessing the economic inequality and the imbalance of power within the society. But this scheme, if very compact, brings out another important issue which, in my opinion, has to be considered. It may be noted that the consumption account (row 4, column D of the Matrix) sets out in the row the added values of the two sectors (Y_M and Y_V) and in the column the consumption of the population in the two types of goods (C_M and C_V), where both Y_V and C_V, non-market aggregates, refer to social value produced and used that does not take

---

[19] As is well-known, switching from representation of the economic process to theoretical explanation of the reproduction mode of a society requires the integration of the accounting scheme with specific assumptions about the behaviour of the two sectors (market and non-market) in the pursuit of their own objectives (profit and well-being). *A fortiori*, in the interpretation of the real world processes, these assumptions must be calibrated to the specific institutional features, considering that, in the different capitalist societies, not only the internal mechanisms in the market and the non-market are different in time and space, but also the boundaries between them (as the continuous pressure on value goods and common goods by the privatisation process shows).

monetary form. This does not mean these aggregates are not 'true' values; it simply means that in the market economy social organisation must find the social forms to redistribute the monetary income to ensure the existence and efficiency of these essential, value-good productive activities. Concrete examples of these redistribution procedures, in addition to public administration, are the redistributive forms within families, voluntary contributions to associations and so on. It is also evident that some types of social organisation increase the non-market value-added, while others can depress it: society's organisational form is part of its social capital.

The remaining relations of Matrix 1 are easily understood. Only the resources revaluation/devaluation items ($RV(K_H)$ and $RV(Z_H)$) and therefore $RV(R_H)$, row 8, column H) merit brief consideration. These two items record the changes that affected the various resource stocks for events other than the production process. Unforeseen obsolescence of a firm's productive instruments or an organisational innovation in the productive process that affects their future productivity, but also the effects of earthquakes, floods and nuclear disasters are all events that increase/reduce the quantity and quality of the stock of resources for the production of future well-being independent of the present production process.[20]

Therefore, an understanding of the relationship between growth (of productive capital goods) and development (of the well-being productive resources) cannot leave out the productive structure of the value-goods sector and its interrelationship with the market-goods sector. In case of changes in the resources devoted to this sector, or in their productive structure, or in complementarity or substitutability between the market and the value-goods sector, it seems plausible to argue that the society's development path can be significantly altered. The representation of the economic process that results from accepting sustainable well-being as a key-concept of economic analysis highlights the causal, circular and cumulative relationship between the social sphere and the market sphere. Even though the possibility of applying a quantitative measure to the aggregates that arise from this analytical choice is fairly remote, it is, nevertheless, not conceptually possible for the economist to exclude from his considerations the structural interdependence that exists between economy and society and to rely on an *a priori* unidirectional (synthetic) effect from one to another that ignores the cumulative effects of their interdependence.

---

[20] It is to be noted that, unlike the current national accounts, net investment expenditure does not generally correspond to an increase in the resources of the country; in fact (identities 6F and 7G), gross investments offset the loss of production efficiency of capital (GI^K_M and GI^K_V) and of the resources (GI^Z_M and GI^Z_V) due both to the production process (e.g. due to pollution, the costs of which are respectively included in D^K_M and in D^Z_M and D^Z_V) but also to other external events (e.g. due to disasters, whose costs are respectively included in $RV(K_H)$ and in $RV(Z_H)$).

Neglecting this analytical dimension precludes possession of the requisite tools for understanding the non-uniqueness between the level of product and the level of well-being. In particular, if we take into account the point that, with reference to the scheme used, the current GDP aggregate is given by the sum $Y_M + B_{MV} + D^Z_M$, then, in present accounting data, since the last two terms are not recorded, the contribution of the market-goods sector to net creation of social value Y_M (by approximation, the GDP current estimate) is systematically overestimated. It is on the strength of this consideration that I can assert the existence of an impasse in (present) economic research since, on the one hand, its concept of 'product' (and the corresponding conceptual scheme) is an inadequate tool for analysing the reality to be studied, while on the other hand, its concept of 'well-being' (and its conceptual scheme) is not a well-developed tool for the persuasive analysis of many major issues. However, if taken seriously, this cognitive tension may be an incentive to organise (and revise) an economic approach able to interpret the economic (and social) process in a more convincing manner.

5.   … And the Implications for Economic Policy

Possessing a more extensive and comprehensive analytical framework for the many qualitative factors in the interaction between economy and society is not only crucial for economic analysis; it is an even more relevant and urgent issue for assessment of the effects of economic policy. In fact, policy prescriptions can be formulated with reference to a conceptual framework based on the 'product' only if we hold the unlikely belief that the structure of relations linking the product to well-being and the composition of productive resources remains stable over time. Once we recognise that the social, political and cultural process serving the material and moral reproduction of society evolve over time, changing the structure of economic and social development, we are compelled to suggest that, in the absence of adequate availability of the necessary information, we do not know enough and therefore the economic policy should be formulated under an explicit *precaution principle*.[21]

We cannot assess the effectiveness of economic policy choices if, centred only on results in terms of product, they do not take into account the effects on the production of value-goods (and their retroactive effects). If it is possible to envisage, on the basis of this framework integrated by realistic assumptions on the different social sectors behaviour, a plurality of developmental trajectories characterised by different

---

[21] There is an extensive and growing economic and social literature regarding the determinants and the effects of the production of what I name value-goods. A (partial) survey of these studies demonstrating the attention from leading scholars this research field already enjoys is set out in Gnesutta (2010).

compositions of product and well-being, then we cannot rely on an economic policy pursuing its results in terms of only product, because the value-goods production and consumption would be strongly undervalued. It is not difficult to understand, for instance, that the 'austerity policies' adopted for a growing market product may produce a negative social effect; again, and as present events are showing, the (expected) increase in a country's GDP can be accompanied by an increase in degradation of resources, by deterioration of working conditions in terms of rights and dignity, by increased collective insecurity due to deterioration of social relations and so on. And, in such cases, we are in very big trouble, since we have no tools to analyse and compare what we gain with the product increase against what we lose with the decrease of well-being.

This necessary caution does not apply only to our insufficient knowledge of how the factors that affect the social and civil progress of a country operate, but indeed, also to the very identification of this term. We must not overlook the fact that 'well-being' is a multidimensional concept that rests on value judgments, not only on which elements of well-being should be considered, but also on which of them loom larger at a given moment in any one particular historical society. There may be several aggregate definitions of quality of life that reflect different political perspectives and the questions they address; in fact, as sustainability involves the future, these varying definitions relate not only to what the future may hold, but even more to what society we want to build. Choosing between different interpretations of sustainable well-being deriving from value judgments is ultimately a normative decision.[22]

The value judgments are not the only normative factor. The need to relate the actions of current economic (and social) policy to the results of a future economic (and social) structure inevitably means that decisions based on such projections are made in a context of fundamental uncertainty. Different possible paths for future conditions of well-being stem from the model applied to describe future interactions, the assumptions as to individual behaviours, including those of the policy makers, the weight given to various factors and the magnitude of future external shocks. Economic policy is then forced to operate with alternative scenarios to assess future states of the economy and society, to be evaluated on the basis of assessment of the risk that such scenarios may prove mistaken. Essentially, also from the theoretical point of view, assuming the sustainability condition means proceeding with explicit predictions of future economic trajectories and with (explicit or implicit) normative choices on values attached to what is to be sustained, and for whom. The fact is that there are very different views on all of these points, not

---

[22] 'However, as what we measure shapes what we collectively strive to pursue – and what we pursue determines what we measure – the report and its implementation may have a significant impact on the way in which our societies look at themselves and, therefore, on the way in which policies are designed, implemented and assessed' (Stiglitz, Sen, Fitoussi 2009, p. 9).

only ideological, but also due to different beliefs about probability distributions of future scenarios.[23] This context raises a clear problem for democracy, concerning who decides the future of society, and how. There is no doubt that the definition of the appropriate forms of a wider democracy still requires theoretical and institutional investigation, but that does not negate the urgency of recognising that economic policy decisions are not only economic, but also social and cultural choices, and therefore cannot be delegated to the cultural hegemony of a technocracy conditioned by the 'fetish' of GDP.

6. To Widen Our Research Space

The difficulty of obtaining a complete picture of economy-society interactions calls into question the coordinates within which economic analysis is currently constrained, not to mention economic policy itself. Taking as significant the interactions between the moral and material reproduction of society without being able to give them a quantitative dimension, albeit approximate and conventional, is a factor that weakens economic analysis and implies the necessity of subjecting economic policy choices to deliberative processes, whereby people can, in severely problematic situations, democratically identify the perspectives that most directly bear on their present and future living conditions. This is the fundamental knot that economists must either cut or untangle – it does not matter how approximate their initial solutions may be – in order to arrive at a more comprehensive evaluation of the progress of society and to achieve a more profound verification of the effects of economic policies.

Acknowledgements

An earlier version of the paper was commented on by Francesco Sarracino and Jordi Mundò; I thank them for very valuable suggestions that allowed me improving my note. The usual disclaimer applies.

---

[23] As we have already seen, it is advisable that, in evaluating the alternatives, the economic policies take into account the worst case scenario, in accordance with the 'precaution principle'.

Appendix: The (Socio-)Economic Relations Network

The accounting identities

1 A	Wealth-Resources: initial stocks :	$K_H^i + Z_H^i$	$= R_H^i$
2 B	Production: market goods:	$B_{VM} + C_M + GI_M^K + GI_M^Z$	$= B_{MV} + Y_M + D_M^K + D_M^Z$
3 C	Production: value goods:	$B_{MV} + C_V + GI_V^K + GI_V^Z$	$= B_{VM} + Y_V + D_V^Z$
4 D	Consumption:	$Y_M + Y_V$	$= C_M + C_V + S_H$
5 E	Wealth accumulation:	$R_H^i + S_H + RV(R_H)$	$= R_H^f$
6 F	Firm's capital formation:	$D_M^K + K_H^f$	$= K_H^i + GI_M^K + GI_V^K + RV(K_H)$
7 G	HES resources formation:	$D_M^Z + D_V^Z + Z_H^f$	$= Z_H^i + GI_M^Z + GI_V^Z + RV(Z_H)$
8 H	Wealth-resources: revaluation:	$RV(K_H) + RV(Z_H)$	$= RV(R_H)$
9 I	Wealth-Resources: final stocks:	R_H^f	$= K_H^f + Z_H^f$

The content of symbols

B_{MV} intermediate value goods in market goods production
B_{VM} intermediate market goods in value goods production
C_M consumption of market goods
C_V consumption of value goods
D_M^K depreciation of firm's capital in market goods production
D_M^Z depreciation of HES resources in market goods production
D_V^Z depreciation of HES resources in value goods production
GI_M^K firm's capital formation in market goods production
GI_V^K firm's capital formation in value goods production
GI_M^Z HES resources formation in market goods production
GI_V^Z HES resources formation in value goods production
K_H^f stock of final firm's capital
K_H^i stock of initial firm's capital
R_H^f stock of final wealth
R_H^i stock of initial wealth
$RV(K_H)$ revaluation of initial stock of firm's capital
$RV(R_H)$ revaluation of initial stock of wealth
$RV(Z_H)$ revaluation of initial stock of HES resources
S_H savings
Y_M added value in market goods production

Y_V added value in value goods production
Z_H^f stock of final HES resources
Z_H^i stock of initial HES resources

References

Eisner, R. (1988) 'Extended Accounts for National Income and Product'. *The Journal of Economic Literature*, 4., Vol. XXVI, December

Fleurbaey, M. (2009) 'Beyond GDP: The Quest for a Measure of Social Welfare'. *The Journal of Economic Literature*, 4.

Gnesutta, C. (1983) *Lineamenti di contabilità economica nazionale*. La Nuova Italia Scientifica, Roma, 1983.

Gnesutta, C. (2010) *Benessere e capitale sociale. Categorie "sostenibili" per l'analisi economica?* in Bonifati G., Simonazzi A. (a cura di), "Il ritorno dell'Economia Politica. Saggi in ricordo di Fernando Vianello". Roma: Donzelli, 2010, pp. 219-240.

Gnesutta, C. (2013) 'Sustainable Well-being as an Economic Indicator: A Challenge for Economic Analysis'. *Rivista italiana degli economisti - The Journal of the Italian Economic Association*, 3.

ISTAT (2013) *Rapporto Bes 2013: il benessere equo e sostenibile in Italia*. Roma: Istat (http://www.istat.it/it/archivio/84348)

Nordhaus, W. and Tobin, J. (1973) 'Is Growth Obsolete?'. *The Measurement of Economic and Social Performance, Studies in Income and Wealth, National Bureau of Economic Research*, vol. 38.

Stiglitz, J.E., Sen, A. and Fitoussi, J-P. (2009) *Report by the Commission on the Measurement of Economic Performance and Social Progress.* (http://www.stiglitz-sen-fitoussi.fr/documents/rapport_anglais.pdf)

Vanoli, A. (2010) 'On the Report by the Commission on the Measurement of Economic Performance and Social Progress (2009). The viewpoint of a retired national accountant'. Paper presented at the 13th Conference of the "*Association de Comptabilité nationale*", 2-4 June 2010, Paris
(http://www.insee.fr/en/insee-statistique-publique/colloques/acn/pdf13/texte-vanoli.pdf)

SUGGESTED CITATION:

Gnesutta, C. (2014) 'If "Well-Being" is the Key Concept in Political Economy…'. *Economic Thought*, 3.2, pp.70-81.
http://www.worldeconomicsassociation.org/files/journals/economicthought/WEA-ET-3-2-Gnesutta.pdf

www.ingramcontent.com/pod-product-compliance
Lightning Source LLC
Chambersburg PA
CBHW051338200326
41519CB00026B/7465